The Media
Against Democracy

The Media
Against Democracy

Thomas Field

Winchester, UK
Washington, USA

First published by Zero Books, 2015
Zero Books is an imprint of John Hunt Publishing Ltd., Laurel House, Station Approach,
Alresford, Hants, SO24 9JH, UK
office1@jhpbooks.net
www.johnhuntpublishing.com
www.zero-books.net

For distributor details and how to order please visit the 'Ordering' section on our website.

Text copyright: Thomas Field 2014

ISBN: 978 1 78099 821 3
Library of Congress Control Number: 2014949685

A CIP catalogue record for this book is available from the British Library.

Design: Lee Nash

Printed and bound by CPI Group (UK) Ltd, Croydon, CR0 4YY, UK

We operate a distinctive and ethical publishing philosophy in all
areas of our business, from our global network of authors to
production and worldwide distribution.

CONTENTS

Introduction

Anarchic Democracy
and the State of the Media

Let's look into our TV screens at one point in our still quite new 21st century, a day after "riots" have taken place in Croydon, London. The production team is obviously hurrying a journalist. Everything is a bit chaotic. She begins by asking: "*Marcus Dowe*, were you shocked by what you've seen there last night?"[1]

This is the voice of the BBC – the model institution for much of the world's media. We see a journalist apparently with earphones in. It is pretty evident that she is getting advice from the backrooms – one bit of which is that her next interviewee is ready. However she has got his name wrong, it's actually *Darcus Howe*, not *Marcus Dowe*. Darcus Howe is a reasonably well-known UK writer and broadcaster. During the course of the brief interchange her interviewee is extremely critical of the state of the nation.[2] It's a place of racist police stops and searches, which the mainstream of British political opinion (including the mainstream media) has paid scant attention to, and this racism is part of a set of conditions that are the context for the "riots."[3] The tone of the interview soon becomes aggressive and starts to verge on the cacophonous. By the end of it the journalist is very certain of something about Mr Howe (even if she was uncertain of his name just a minute ago) – he is an experienced rioter! She continues: "Mr Howe, if I can just ask you – you are not a stranger to riots yourself... you have taken part in them yourself." Howe replies – obviously angered by this suggestion – that he has never rioted but he has been on plenty of demonstrations.[4] Please could the interviewer have some respect? At this point and without any acknowledgement of Howe's request, let alone anything resembling an apology, the interview is suddenly terminated and the BBC24 news channel rolls on. And on and on.

Howe's is a voice of dissent – what is interesting is that this voice from the demos is disdainfully struck down by the powers that be at the BBC. This is a Homeric anti-democratic moment. As Rancière points out, this hatred of democracy has ancient provenance. Here is Homer, as referenced by Rancière in *Ten Theses on Politics*: "If they insist on speaking out, Ullysees will strike anyone belonging to the demos in the back with his sceptre." In this interview we are prevented from hearing what Howe is saying. Rancière again: "To be of the demos is to be outside of the count, to have *no speech* to be heard." So the Homeric sceptre comes out and the backstabbing event occurs, as the journalist publically accuses Howe of being a rioter himself. He therefore has no right to speak, they assume, exactly as Rancière emphasises. "The one who belongs to the demos, who speaks when he is not to speak, is the one who partakes in what he has no part in." So of course the interview is suddenly terminated!

Another moment, about a month earlier. Another old man. He wants to make a statement to his questioners but his request is refused. The old man, and his son, who accompanies him, look somewhat peeved. The first question is put; the son begins to answer the questions. The old man is unhappy at all this and decides he will make part of the statement anyway and so in an apparent act of spontaneity the son is interrupted, the old man speaks: "This is the most humble day of my life," he begins.

This is Rupert Murdoch, the voice of News Corporation – one of the most lucrative profit-driven global multi-media institutions. Murdoch is not humble enough to be told when he can and when he can't make statements by elected members of the UK parliament. (We are at the hearing of the Culture, Media and Sports Select Committee of British MPs into the News Corporation phone-hacking scandal – July 2011.)[5] As the interrogation continues he finds it difficult to answer the questions that the MPs are posing. There are long pauses as he apparently tries to recollect the necessary facts.

What conclusions can we draw from these contrasting media events? First, class power matters: someone (Darcus Howe) speaking apparently as part of the unrepresented "rioters" gets short shrift from the powers that be – in this case the BBC. He is allotted time, berated, insulted and switched off as the institution requires. However when someone speaks from a position of corporate power (Murdoch) they get their way no matter what the elected try to do.

Second, what you see with Darcus Howe is that when the "part that has no part,"[6] to use Jacques Rancière's expression, tries to speak then it doesn't get listened to; but not only that. What Howe has to say is not only attacked by those who attempt to control our understanding of democratic events but it is also a matter of being able to perceive or not to perceive what he says – his contribution is made nigh on inaudible by the talking over and questioning of the interviewer. So although there are longstanding critiques of media practice based on issues of bias or misrepresentation I suggest that a more fundamental and telling critical understanding of "the media" should be based around questions of the visible and the non-visible or the perceivable and the non-perceivable. This is a matter of, as Rancière has it, *aesthesis*.[7]

Third, there is such a thing as capitalist and corporate media power: in one instance (Darcus Howe) it stops the expression of a voice; in the other (Rupert Murdoch) it forces through expression of its corporate statement.

Fourth, we cannot necessarily expect the state or state broadcasters to be democratic. So talk of a democratic British Spring, (as there was, at the time of the hearing) just because of the existence of "public service broadcasting," and of parliamentary interrogation and government enquiry, is always going to be vastly exaggerated.

These examples (and other events) illustrate that it is high time to interrogate the relationship between the media and democracy. This will necessitate a number of attendant questions. My method will be philosophy-based rather than (what some call) theory-based. So I will use concepts from the philosophical tradition such as ontology; those from the tradition of political philosophy; and those from the Socratic tradition of trying to define the concepts that we take for granted but may not be capable of explaining – "justice" being one such concept. But here I want us to critically address concepts of democracy and of media. So how will we proceed? By a number of interconnected enquiries.

1. What is there to make images and sounds of? This is an ontological question.
2. What is the meaning of "democracy"?
3. What do we mean by this term "media"?
4. What happens when "the media" tries to put "democracy" onto our screens?
5. What are the preconditions for the creation of emancipatory images and sounds?

These five questions, and answers to them, are what this book is about. I want to briefly outline the direction I will take and the reasons why these enquiries are crucial.

1. Our "democratic" situation

We have the lamentable state of Western capitalist politics and its emptying out of the significance of democracy – testified to by the oligarchical[8] nature of the states themselves, the homogenisation of mainstream and dominant political discourse[9] and, fairly recently, the technocratic appropriation of nominal European democracies in Greece and Italy. The latter events imply that what we had been calling "democracy" was in fact nothing of the sort and was something valueless and empty. In fact it was disposable – overnight! This is where the maintenance of "democratic" insignificance has eventually got us. We have hit the rock bottom of capitalist-parliamentary democracy and it is from this foundational perspective that we can begin to ask about the meaning of democracy; and it is just this question that forms one of the two main axes of this book.

Whereas much anglo-analytic political philosophy is about how to maintain "democratic" state institutions, which sometimes only adds up to a sort of rarefied policy wonkery, there is an alternative radical strand of predominantly European thought which demonstrates that democracy is in fact not at all a state form,[10] so we shouldn't over-value attempts to "improve" oligarchical state "democracy." In trying to understand these notions from a questioning and radical perspective we can turn to, for example: Rancière's notion of anarchic democracy[11]; Abensour's argument that democracy is against the state[12]; and Nancy's political neo-ontological argument that the existence of democracy necessitates the anarchic.[13]

2. Our media situation

At the start of 2014 the apparent embarrassment of News Corporation is abating[14] but nothing has really happened to its power base – even if it has got rid of one of its "toxic" titles and a key member of its staff (Andy Coulson) has ended up in jail. The outcome of all this is that the state has done nothing to change the media order of the UK where News Corporation is dominant. Indeed it seems the state is aligned with News Corporation against the UK judicial processes.[15] The media order in the UK (as well as around the world) is oligopolistic – is one where there is much power in few hands.

In the realm of "The Media" utter the word "democracy" and get unending support from political powers; utter the word "anarchy" and get arrested! "The Media" tells us that X-state *descends* into anarchy and that Y-state may be able to attain the *heights* of democracy. This book will explain why "The Media" gets the relationship between anarchy and democracy wrong – over and over again.

Any future politics will be played out in the streets and in the squares but also through things like television, radio and the internet etc. I am sceptical of the term "media" – we have to be aware of what Nietzsche calls the subterfuge of language and of the way that a term like this, which was first coined speculatively,[16] does later become an eternal conceptual verity. We need a genealogy of the discourse which has as its key term "media," and this book marks the start of such an analysis.

In the case of "The Media" we have to emphasise that the term has a history. It was born in the wake of early twentieth-century revolution and general strikes in the 1920s – just as the ur-media institution of the BBC established itself, simultaneously creating a new kind of public sphere and a new myth of representation. So we must interrogate just what "The Media" is and what it does when democracy happens.

Just as Western states are oligarchic, Western media is oligopolistic. In both these realms there is immense power in few hands. So in political discourse we are justified in calling the order of political power "The State" and in calling the order of communicative power "The Media."

3. The question of mediation

What will be argued is that "The Media" does not mediate. In other words this is a not only an attack on "The Media" but also a general attack on how the discourse of Media Studies with its key concept of mediation has approached no matter what event, but especially democratic events. "Media Studies" is a spectacularly successful discourse in terms at least of its ability to multiply itself; over the last 25 years or so the academic subject has proliferated on both sides of the Atlantic and around the world. But my argument is that "Media Studies" has failed to understand its subject and has indeed maintained a situation in which we no longer understand what is happening when there is "media" activity. So by maintaining ignorance, this "radical" academic activity – the one we call "Media Studies" – ends up supporting oligarchical rule.

4. Image culture

What kind of image culture could there be after the age of mediation? After Castoriadis I stress the value of images and sounds that are "windows upon the chaos."[17] These would not be mediations, but ways of understanding that what is *is* chaos and creation, and that democratic living is creative living on the edge of chaos.

Chapter One

The End of the Media

What do we mean when we talk about "The Media"? Why did we start talking about it? Will we talk about it in a 100 years time? It is presently extremely difficult to stop using this term. (We could say that it may be easier to imagine the end of the world than it is to imagine the end of the media.) But we will have to stop at some point if, as I will argue, the media – both as a concept and as we seem to know it – is against democracy, and democracy is at the heart of any emancipatory politics.[18] And if we want to live, other than as pigs, then freedom and equality – democratic living, in short – is essential.

Some things don't seem to have beginnings, and the media is one of them. Some histories of the media use the term as if it existed at least since antiquity. Saturated as we are by what is called the media, it is no surprise that we find it difficult to think properly about its history. Once we do think through the history of the media properly then we can know both that "the media" can end, and why democratic politics will end it.

The relationship between media and politics is one of perennial outcry and protest from both the powerful and the apparent powerless. Beyond the totting up of political party screen time with a stopwatch how can this relationship be properly understood? We can start by asking: what does it actually mean to mediate? What is apparently being mediated? Then we can ask what *could* effectively mediate or represent democracy?[19]

Where might we find answers to such questions? What resources are available for a critical study of the relationship between media and democracy? Some would suggest "Media Studies"; however Media Studies has become (has always

1

been?[20]) a type of one-dimensional thinking that has produced and sustained a number of myths and misapprehensions often built around false dichotomies (which I discuss shortly) about the relationship between images and power and democracy, and which has had little effect on the object it critically studies. Media practitioners have looked upon Media Studies with a sense of bafflement, and in one way they are right to. They think they are mediating and so does Media Studies – so what's the fuss about if the two sides agree upon that? However my argument is that it would be better for us all if we just jettisoned the term "media" completely in relation to the production of audio-visual cultures; it is a term of fairly recent application and we should consider alternative ways of discussing these cultures, without this term.

So to return to the initial question, what do we mean when we refer to "the media"? And what is mediation? Meanings usually attributed to the word, apart from the ones associated with communication, are likely to reference something about occupying some middle position or being regarded as interme-diate. But then we should ask: "intermediate" between exactly what and what? As a verb, mediate could be said to mean to settle some dispute as an intermediary between parties, or to act between parties to effect an agreement, compromise or reconcili-ation. It is my contention that this concept and the practices that accompany it are profoundly anti-political and therefore anti-democratic. What I mean by "the political" derives from some of Chantal Mouffe's thinking about it. Using her work it is possible to see how the media has an anti-democratic effect and how it occults the reality of the political, which is that in any society there is and there always will be a dimension of political antag-onism that cannot be eradicated. For me this is linked to the notion of ontological chaos which I develop later in the book.

So the first reason I am giving for the conclusion that the media is against democracy is that the media as mediator would deny what Mouffe has called "the nature of the political" and "the dimension of radical negativity that manifests itself in the ever-present possibility of antagonism."[21] A true account of political-social relations would have to require a "coming to terms with the lack of a final ground and the undecidability that pervades every order." The lack of any final ground is therefore a radically negative ontological non-state. I will conceptualise this as political chaos (not a term that Mouffe uses). But for now we can say, with Mouffe, that any settlement that would have to be the result of some kind of mediation would deny that the settlement is always characterised by a particular set of power relations and so also an attempt to cover over the future possibility of antagonism. So mediation and the proposed settlement that goes with it must always to some extent try to mask the "sedimented hegemonic practices" that brought it about. Therefore the concept of "mediation" is opposed to counter-hegemonic practices which are democratic by nature and so the concept of the media is opposed to the idea of democracy.

My second reason for the conclusion that the media is against democracy is that it pretends to mediate something but it is unable to mediate anything. This is because if what is *is* chaos then what is there for the media to mediate? I am going to suggest that if we privilege a thinking of being as chaos or *hyper-chaos* then this may provide us with a means to live more democratically. If it is true that what is *is* chaos then the producers of new images and sounds would have to accept that nothing is given[22] (which is emphatically not to say that nothing exists). The producers of sounds and images would have to accept that mediation of a given as a real is impossible, or at best illusory. To the extent that they deny chaos then they also deny the conditions of democratic thinking and action.

For these two reasons we must accept that the media is against democracy and so we should welcome the end of the media.

It is possible to analyse our current cultural-political situation once we take on board this critical account of the media and mediation. So to start off here are eight truths about our audio-visual culture that indicate problems with the concept of mediation.

1. Cultural power does exist

By cultural power I mean the capacity of the nexus of global multi-media conglomerates and state-directed public service broadcasting systems (the oligopoly that is the global media industry) to shape our ideas about what there is and what it means, and such activity is wrongly described as mediation.[23] The revelations at the British *Leveson Enquiry*[24] indicate the use of such power by, for example: News Corporation to attempt to blackmail John Major's Conservative UK government into changing policy on the EU; its efforts to try to get Blair's Labour government, as well as Chirac's French government, to join the Iraq War coalition; and the placement of one of their men (Andy Coulson – later found guilty, in July 2014, of illegal journalistic practices) at the heart of Cameron's 2010 onwards Conservative government.

2. There is no such thing as the media

If we consider the institutions that produce the images and sounds and broadcast them to a public then in what sense can this global oligopoly convincingly situate itself as a mediator? Somewhere in between, on neutral ground? A settling presence? It appears not. Even if it seems to have been ever-present in its ever-presence, the media and the concept "the media" were born at a particular moment – in the 1920s.[25] This was just after the world-historical communist event in Russia and around the time of the socialism of The General Strike in the UK, which the BBC played such an important part in by "siding with the government" against the strikers. Around this time of public social class conflict the term "the media" was coined by those on the side of the powerful – the advertisers. That radical activists and thinkers have pretty much totally taken up this term "the media," a term coined by their adversaries, may well one day be considered as one of the ironies of history.

If we simply ask the ontological question "what is it there to mediate?" then something starts to unravel. Francois Jullien[26] describes a scene we are all probably familiar with. The tourist alights with camera in hand, takes a photograph and returns relieved to their seat. What is it that they are relieved about?

It's clear: they are relieved to have avoided coming face to face – coming face to face with that which presents itself to them, engulfing their attention, and which overwhelms them.[27]

There is of course a whole set of implicit practices involved in the taking of a tourist snap resulting in the "realisation" of a set of "acquired codifications." Now imagine this use of a set of acquired codifications multiplied a hundredfold, and you will perhaps be able to understand what is happening in this, another familiar scene: a journalist, a camera and a sound recorder in front of the site of some kind of event. It seems to be claimed that *being there* guarantees that we (their audience) get to *what there is,* that this can simply be transmitted to an audience. Such practices are an attempt to try to bolster an imaginary media role as guardian of "the knowledge," by being present at the ostensible site of the event. The producers imagine and hope that the audience also imagines that mere presence provides some cognitive connection – "here is our correspondent outside number 10, at the factory, at the police station" etc. The news team return to their car relieved they have their footage.

In relation to the lone photographer example, Jullien quotes (and translates) Heraclitus: "without intelligence, having listened, to the deaf they resemble; this saying bears witness to them: present they are absent."[28] As Jullien emphasises, they don't encounter. "They are there, physically present, in flesh and bone, but have, as they say, the mind elsewhere, that is to say in fact nowhere: dispersed, dissipated, unproductive: not awakened."[29] Present, they are absent – they do not encounter.

The film maker Michelangelo Frammartino[30] affirms this Jullienesque anti-mediationalism but also suggests an alternative way of thinking the relationship between camera and what there is. The camera "is not simply a tool for reproducing reality, but I feel it is a tool with the ability to perceive, to capture, to film the bond between man and nature, that invisible thing that is in between... the thing that binds man to these other elements. It somehow manages to point this out to us and make it come alive." His film, *Le Quattro Volte*, is set in Calabria, Italy, but his project in the film is not to represent Calabria. Rather Calabria is "present" in his work. "It's something that happens without me actually aiming to tell its whole story." So his film is an exercise in "the humility of the eye." The French film maker Robert Bresson, in his Notes on the cinematographer, seems to agree with Frammartino. "A mechanism gives rise to the unknown and not because one has found this unknown in advance." And Frammartino is not hesitant in pointing out the political consequences of his film and his use of images – it is because Silvio Berlusconi came to power partly through the control of images that Frammartino wanted to produce images "that gave the audience freedom."

If we to start to develop ontological questions about what there is,[31] then it becomes possible to recognise that what gets elided in notions of mediation are the following prospects: in the words of Castoriadis the idea "that what is *is* chaos"; in the words of Meillassoux that there is ontological hyper-chaos and radical contingency; in the words of Badiou that beyond what is presented there could be something of the evental; and finally in the words of Jullien that what there is could facilitate what he calls *l'essor* – meaning "the flight" – in the most positive senses of the word.[32] Media practice and Media Studies' absolutely key concept of mediation occults these chaotic, evental and ontological possibilities.

3. Media audiences do not "choose" their readings and media audiences are not "affected"

Either audiences simply choose meanings or they get an overpoweringly negative charge from the media, debilitating them in one way or another. Both sides of this false dichotomy occult the force or *potentia* of the image: one in denial, the other in puritanical disgust and paranoia. Rather than go with either side, could we not instead consider another possibility that what the media sometimes offers us is a never totally successful attempt to cleanse its images and sounds of the chaotic and the evental. The concept of mediation neutralises and eviscerates the chaotic and the evental. As do codes of media professionalism which are very tightly drawn around what is an acceptable image or sound, so excluding that which is in some way excessive of those codifications. At the same time political assumptions look right past those happenings which could be events (let's say for now in Badiou's sense of the term[33]) but are somehow beyond or outside of their expectations, or conceptual schemes.

I sketch later just what a chaotic offer could be like, where the experience offered is one of the chaotic and the evental rather than that of the packaged media practice or an assumed choice of meaning. What is obliterated in the discourse of differential readings and of media effects is the *potentia* of the image, and the experience, however opaque, of its obscure, but real power to link to the chaotic.

4. The media is not democratic

How can quasi-state bodies like public service broadcasters, and profit-driven corporations which are in any case dominated by a fraction of the bourgeoisie,[35] be counted as somehow representative of democracy?[36] Or even neutral mediators between competing social groups?

5. The Media Industries are class institutions

Who works for the media institutions? Class, in the 2010s – the social variable that may finally be re-emerging after a period of occultation, when we were all bourgeois – is the most useful sociological concept for working towards an answer to this question. It particularly struck home to me as I watched the BBC's *Newsnight* flagship programme as a presumably democratic discussion was going on about Gideon Oliver Osborne's (also known as George Osborne, Chancellor of the Exchequer of the British state) 2012 UK budget between Allegra and Jeremy (a *Newsnight* journalist and an anchorman respectively). Not only are the names significant but also the accents and the *habitus*. Why this concentration of the bourgeoisie in the age of apparent equal opportunities? Suffice to recall a very illuminating article in *The Guardian* a few years back about how graduates get employed in the British media.[37] It is no longer enough to offer to work for free, there are far too many graduates offering to be slaves! Now you must go beyond slavery and actually pay the media company to work for them. The resultant media class could therefore, for the most part, only be the rich self-appointed mediators of the officially political, itself dominated by the rich. Showbiz kids making movies of themselves...

6. The media is not autonomous

Either it is profit-driven so driven by the laws of the market, or it is in fear of whatever government fixes its funding mechanism therefore driven by the rules of the state. (And what if somebody suggested that the media was relatively autonomous? Can this conceptual monstrosity exist anyway?) So in what kind of position is the media to be neutral mediators?

The BBC's flagship presenters snarl like rottweilers at politicians whilst its DGs get sacked or called to ministerial offices for their instructions (Greg Dyke and Mark Thompson, respectively). This exposes the problem of the Paxman method – the creation of much heat and little light, fabricating the idea of a genuine BBC democratic interrogation. Did that infamous minister (Conservative Michael Howard) overrule his administrator? Did he even threaten to? We still don't even know. Years later both interviewer and interviewee appear on a self-congratulatory BBC self-assessment joking and laughing about the incident confirming a suspicion that all that snarling and respondent prevarication is part of an oligarchic game.

7. The media does not produce texts
and

8. The media does not produce images that do not have power[38]

If we go back to Barthesian basics and examine the concept of a text, which again is key to Media Studies thinking, then what do we find but that such concepts as text, meaning, representation, polysemy etc. downplay the force of the image. Better is the later Barthes of *Camera Lucida* who makes his confessions about his past misunderstandings when he tries to approach the force of the image with his concept of the *punctum*. I say he approaches it because he cannot quite adequately conceptualise it, finally sinking into an autobiographical subjective sacralisation of the disorder of the "prick" of the image. What he does emphasise is the disorderliness of certain experiences in front of images, which is valuable and I will develop some thinking on this disorderliness later. However for now suffice to say that the textual critic in Barthes cannot help but fetishise the text, in this case the photograph, cutting it off from the rest of what exists.

My argument will be that we cannot properly understand the disorder Barthes alludes to without again resituating the image within the ontological. Unfortunately semiotic concepts as used in the dominant Cultural Studies tradition only imagine media that offers meanings. This tradition then limits its conception of audience responses to either taking up the semantic offers or rejecting them – as if in a marketplace of meanings and images – so that audiences are able to mould texts into a preferred readings and are able simply, sometimes, to take them or reject them. Other possibilities, other than the so-called negotiated and oppositional readings, cannot be, or are not, conceptualised in terms of their positive power, for example as apprehensions of the evental or as windows upon the chaos; rather they are theorised simply as mediations, empty, eviscerations of the real.[39]

George Simmel has said that: "Life is ineluctably condemned to become reality only in the guise of its opposite, that is as form."[40] I am proposing that rather than use the language of media, text, meaning and, most importantly, mediation, which has become the mainstay of mainstream Media Studies, a more critical account of the media may be sustained if we forget mediation and instead use "form" to describe the produce of most "media" work. We might say following Simmel that social and political life, when appropriated by the media and produced as a "form" by it, becomes the opposite of itself – as form it is detached from the "force that created it... going well beyond its detachment and turning back against life," suggests Miguel Abensour.[41] How would this happen? Abensour suggests it is because of the conflicts between life and form. Life: "dynamism, the continuous flux of experience, impulsion, overflowing spontaneity." Form: "a crystallisation that acts as a power of conservation in view of maintaining the cohesion of the whole." Later Abensour returns to Simmel quoting again, "as life continues they [forms] tend to become inflexible and remote from life, indeed hostile to it."

However what escapes form or is beyond form and which is existent is still the vivid, ecstatic and chaotic nature of democratic events. In order to understand democracy we have to have a new understanding of what a democratic event is, of what living is and ultimately, as Francois Jullien has it, a *"philosophie du vivre."*[42] Could thinking about *le vivre* expose the fact that what the cultural industries are doing is pre-dominantly just the production of forms and not the mediation of things? Mark Cousins' excellent TV series *The Story of Film* has an account of a very interesting moment in the film *Medium Cool*. One of the main characters of the film is a television cameraman: "Jesus I love to shoot film," he says. Haskell Wexler, the director comments about this:

> I think he says that because he has a sensory feeling about images but I also think that he says that because it protects him, it gives him an idea of putting things within a frame, it give him an idea of being detached, being an observer, and then being an observer absolves him from being a participant.

Wexler goes on to suggest that there are times when the camera operator may be so unable to stop their participation in an event that they will "have to put the camera down." So the issue, for all of us, may be how to put the camera down, in order that we begin to answer: how can we be present in the world? How can we conserve this feeling of plenitude which surges without warning and centres on the ecstasy of existence...?[43] We might add that to ensure that this is not just an empty ecstasy we need to have it with others – in other words we need to ask about how to have the ecstasy of political existence? We can get near to answering this question and thereby being able to live such an existence if we ask – what is there to have an experience with? More particularly for this book and project – what is there to make images and sounds of? These questions raise issues of ontology and epistemology.

So if we must look at chaos, and offer an understanding of it, this will necessitate some philosophical exposition and comment.

Chapter Two

The Impossibility of Media

In the face of an event where the existence of ourselves or others is put into question we sometimes begin to consider the fact of mortality. At that point we could begin some kind of philosophical deliberation about the value of existence and what we should do while we exist. We become critically existential. That is a valuable moment because the examined life is worth living. But what else can be of value in such an existential moment? Let me ask you what it felt like when you realised that you were mortal? What a vertiginous moment that was?[44] Just why is it that such a moment could be so vertiginous? It is probably because within that mortal thought there lies another one, even more dizzying and astonishing. So much so that our mind recoils from it. In there, beyond an initial egological response, is the thought that not only ourselves but *everything* can cease to be or cease to be as it is, at anytime. Here is the news from Quentin Meillassoux:[45]

> Everything could actually collapse: from trees to stars, from stars to laws, from physical laws to logical laws; and this not by virtue of some superior law whereby everything is destined to perish, but by virtue of the absence of any superior law capable of preserving anything, no matter what, from perishing.[46]

This is what Meillassoux calls "hyper-chaos"[47] and he has a rationalist proof of this ontological chaos. Meillassoux argues that we can have absolute knowledge that what is *is* hyper-chaos. The absolute truth that Meillassoux stresses is **the necessity of contingency** – that there is an absence of necessary reason for the existence of anything.[48] This conclusion is derived from Meillassoux's argument of "correlational facticity." I will spend a little time just briefly setting out some of Meillassoux's arguments.[49]

First of all we have to define Meillassoux's neologism "correlationism." Correlationism is a description of various strands of metaphysics which tend to emphasise the correlation of being and thought. There are weak and strong forms of correlationism. One strong version which Meillassoux calls "subjectalism" absolutises the correlation. A weaker form of correlationism seeks to avoid that particular peril of subjectalism – it wants to counter such an absolutisation of the correlation. In order to do this the weaker form of correlation puts forward the argument of correlational facticity. This consists in maintaining that the correlation is not absolutely necessary and that this absence of an "absolute necessity of correlation" is thinkable. This thinkability can be justified through argument – it is not just an opinion or a faith. The argument rests on the thesis that thinking can think its own absence of necessity as "supra-individual structure." (Meillassoux claims that this can be termed an existential act of thought.) The mode of argument is via negative – nothing about the correlational position indicates its own necessity; "it cannot be proved that this subjective unthinkability of non-correlation corresponds to the absolute impossibility of such a non-correlational reality existing." So correlation is an *arche* fact – "any fact which I cannot, in any way, conceive of as being other than it is, or as not being, but whose necessity I nevertheless cannot prove." So the quality that characterises the correlation is one of *arche*-facticity, given that the necessity of the correlation cannot be proven. The non-necessity of the correlation is supported by the fact that we are capable of thinking our possible non-being and therefore the non-being of the correlation. So we can conclude that there is the possible non-being of everything, including correlation. So correlational facticity – that the correlation is contingent – is an absolute. As a result we can deduce that what is *is* hyper-chaos.

So partly in summary and partly in development of Meillassoux's thought, we continue. And from this point on we can work with the understanding that the correlation as supra-individual structure is itself never in a necessary form; with Meillassoux we accept that any kind of correlation, and the correlation itself, is not necessary. After that we know that what *is* could be very other from what we take it to be. And the thing that we use to understand being, which in itself has being – the correlation mechanism – can itself be very other than what it is at the moment. So the radicalisation of correlationism which Meillassoux undertakes is one that annihilates the necessary and perennial assumed qualities of the correlation. There is no reason for the correlation to be the way it is. Therefore the structure of what is *is* itself contingent – it could be otherwise. There is no non-contingent ordering mechanism; anything can be otherwise at any point.[50]

But hang on, a critical friend might say – everything doesn't seem too chaotic all of the time. So at this point we should really investigate what we could mean by "chaos," which is an issue which Peter Hallward picks up on when he points out:

The plain fact remains, however, that the world we experience does not seem chaotic but stable. But how exactly are we to explain the fact of everyday empirical consistency on the basis of radical contingency and the total absence of causal necessity? If physical laws could actually change for no reason, would it not be extraordinarily improbable if they did not change frequently, not to say frenetically?[51]

Hallward but also Meillassoux seem to have had some problems with the concept of chaos; for example Meillassoux vacillates in naming ontological chaos, sometimes calling it hyper-chaos then calling *surchaos* then back again to hyper-chaos. So for reasons of clarification at this point I think it would be useful to consider the work of another French philosopher who puts chaos at the heart of his ontology. It is in Cornelius Castoriadis' thinking that we find a useful definition that can be used to answer Hallward's question about chaos and help with Meillassoux's uncertainty. For Castoriadis **what is** *is* **chaos**. Could he have put it more starkly than the following?

> The world – being – is essentially Chaos, Abyss, Groundlessness...[52]

Elsewhere he writes:

> "Being" is not a system, is not a system of systems, and is not a great chain. Being is abyss, or chaos, or the groundless... These fundamental facts about being... have been veiled by traditional ontology... because in its dominant stream this ontology worked with the basic hypercategory of determinancy.[53]

These are astounding and important philosophical assertions. What I want to do is to explore the rationale that Castoriadis offers to support them. What does Castoriadis mean by chaos?[54] How does he attempt to uncover the veiling of ontological chaos that he refers to?

In *False and True Chaos*,[55] Castoriadis seeks to establish the differences between his conception of chaos, which he roots in ancient Greek texts, and the kinds of meaning the word has taken on in contemporary use. For Castoriadis chaos does not mean disorder and confusion, which Hallward seems to think it should, but rather the void. (Castoriadis links this original Greek term to two other Greek words: *chaino*, meaning chasm, and *chasko*, meaning to gape.) He concludes that chaos should be taken to mean total indetermination. Thus at this point

Castoriadis takes his leave from the scientific deterministic idea of chaos given in versions of chaos theory popularly understood through the notion of the butterfly effect. Rather, as I said, Castoriadis wants to start off from an understanding of chaos as total indetermination.

Just like Meillassoux, Castoriadis proposes a new ontology in which chaos will be the fundamental notion. Chaos is the without-ground of being; it is part inexhaustibility and part immanent capacity for creation. It is the abyss which is behind every existent; it is that which generates the creation of forms which, much further upstream, so to speak, then present what *is* as cosmos, as order, as organised world. Moreover, and this is crucial for understanding what seems like a paradox, once we try to understand *the* basis of this "cosmos" then it always escapes us. It does this because we cannot reduce one strata of being to another; among the strata there is not one that is fundamental or more elementary. The forms that make up a kind of second-order meaningful world arise out of the chaos but the chaos is not ultimately determining.

This argument is supported by Markus Gabriel, who reaches the following conclusion (which aligns with what Castoriadis argues but without the hint of vitalism sometimes suggested in Castoriadis' work):

We are located in a more than infinite proliferation of fields of sense with no beginning and no end. There is no over-arching structure, no arché governing the whole thing. For one thing, there is no whole thing, no world, but only the frayed plurality of manifold appearing. The world does not exist precisely because everything exists.[56]

Castoriadis sees the flux of what Gabriel would call "fields of sense" in terms of desires and affects and ultimately as creation. But nevertheless this argument for a lack of an over-arching structure by Gabriel is consonant with Castoriadis' position.

When Castoriadis shifts the argument to the psychoanalytical level this shift serves good illustrative purposes. He sets out how the chaos of the *psyche* itself produces a flux of affects and desires, none of which can be reduced to the strata of the physico-chemical. Yet this psychical flux is reworked by human beings to create a "meaningful" everyday world and ultimately a contingently meaningful cosmos. Even if the psyche is an abyss, it is something from out of which an (always provisional) order of some sort is formed. So for Castoriadis, at the heart of the psychic and at the heart of being there is a void, a nothingness. This means that there is no answer to the question of why the universe exists[57] and that any such attempted answer is only added to being by humans who create the "answer" so as to give themselves shelter from chaos. So although we have constructed religious or sociological narratives which attempt to deny this essential void, Castoriadis insists they too must ultimately be put aside – there is no God or Laws of God, or History or Laws of History, to shelter us from the chaos. Significance, sense, mediation, form, even identity, are all also such shelters.

The inacceptability of the void is one of the reasons why things like national identity are held with such importance by certain people – because a denial of this identity threatens to bring forth the chaos of the no-sense[58]; all the effort of the creation of identity and the psychic comfort that it provides could be thrown away and never recuperated. That is why for some, national identity must be maintained and defended at all costs; and it is a key reason why the productions of national broadcasting systems can have such apparent value. It is also why a very disturbing question for some people would be: given that what there is *is* chaos then what is there to identify with? To make sense of? To mediate? What if there is only imaginary identification? What if society itself is an imaginary institution? Is there just imaginary sense, imaginary identification, imaginary mediation? In other words we have to face up to the fragility of our significations, and that they are created out of chaos.

One thing that propels human being to reflect upon itself is its own unceasing ability to create surprising new forms – to create a chaotic flux of forms and presentations which challenge our ideas about our "essence" – so in effect Castoriadis is foregrounding the existential situation of human being. Any "essence" that we may conclude we have must always be considered as provisional, as we are continually challenged and changed by the flux of productions, including productions about what we are. Castoriadis also asks us to consider creations such as the person of Socrates, Wagner's *Tristan und Isolde*, the cathedral at Reims and Ravel's *Gaspard de la nuit,* among others. He draws our attention to the fact these do not just realise the possibilities of a form (unlike a triangle; the various versions of a triangle realise its possibilities but without alteration as to its essence – three straight lines joined etc.). Once they appear then altogether unthinkable and unthought new possibilities are also created, unlike the appearance of a type of triangle or the birth of a new horse which do not produce such new unthought of possibilities. These once-realised possibilities break apart any chains of causality; they are new – they are undeducible and unproducible – therefore not part of a deterministic chain of causes and effects.

To illustrate this idea of the creation of new possibilities Castoriadis gives the example of the creation by Beethoven of the Fifth Symphony:

Is the Fifth Symphony possible at the moment of The Big Bang? Either the question has no meaning or, if it does, the sole response is: it is impossible. The possibility of the Fifth Symphony is posited starting from the moment men create music.[59]

Although the determinist would argue that the creation of music is just one of the moments in the long chain of causes and effects that started with the Big Bang, Castoriadis could respond by arguing that determinism misunderstands not the meaning of being but just what sort of thing being is – being in itself, he argues, is creation. The so-called effect, he may say, in an apparent chain of causes and effects, is itself a moment of creation; it may have a condition but the consequence of that condition is a creation which itself functions as a condition, not a cause, for a new creation and so on.

Castoriadis is very keen to distinguish indeterminacy from creation. Creation is not just indeterminacy, it is also anti-indeterminacy; in fact it is the positing of new determinations. "The French Revolution is *the positing of new determinations*," he writes, "a creation of forms." And here Castoriadis evokes the classic Platonic concept – the idea or *eidos*. "An *eidos* means a set of determinations, a set of possibilities and impossibilities that are defined the moment the form is posited." For an example Castoriadis takes the figure of Socrates:

> Socrates is not Socrates because he is indeterminate but because he determines – through what he says, through what he does, through what he is, through what he makes himself be, and through the way he makes himself die – a type of individual that he embodies and that did not exist beforehand.

Socrates is then a creation and a creator – he marks a point at which human being itself is recreated. Standing a long way back and taking a very long view of human history Castoriadis is able to dramatically exemplify the change in the nature of human being itself as altered by itself and not by a God or any laws of nature or history.

Castoriadis argues that we must recognise the role of imagination as the key quality of human being. It is imagination that has allowed us to be the creators of philosophy. Against and contrary to both the British empiricist tradition of Hume and Locke which minimises the creative role of imagination, and the rationalist Cartesian tradition which diminishes the role of imagination whilst promoting the intellect, Castoriadis conceptualises imagination not as a combinatory faculty (as does the tradition derived from Hume and Locke) but rather as a power of pure invention: the imagination as the capacity to posit a new form. Castoriadis sees the imagination as something other than the result of a combination of sensations (for example, in the anglo tradition the combination of sense data after they hit the Lockean *tabula rasa*) but rather the moment of sensation is itself a moment of imagination and therefore of creation.

Castoriadis uses the example of the creation of colour by the human organism as an example of this moment of sensation/creation:

We can determine a physico-physiological correspondence between certain wavelengths of light and the colour of red or blue; we absolutely cannot "explain" either physically or physiologically the sensation red or blue as to its *quality*... for the *quale* and the tale of the colour, there is no "explanation."

This being, colour, does not exist in nature. In nature, as science tells us, there are only wavelengths; we are the ones that set these wavelengths into something, into image, Castoriadis argues, by an act of imagination.

So imagination is given a primacy in relation to sensation, which is beyond and outside of the empiricist and the rationalist tradition. We are imagining creatures, and this imaginary creature – the human being – imagines on a macro scale too. It follows from the demonstration of creativity at the micro scale that imagination plays the key role even at the macro scale – at the level of the creation of sense from the social world, what he calls "the social imaginary, the instituting imaginary."

So both Meillassoux and Castoriadis argue that being is chaos. We humans live with ontological chaos and anarchy. In relation to the critique of the concept of "the media," which is the overall drive of this book, using Castoriadis we can understand that because of this lack of determinacy we can create not mediations but rather new audio-visual forms.

What is the upshot of this philosophical work – ontological chaos and "mediation"

How can it be possible to mediate chaos (that which is without foundation and is of indeterminacy) – that chaos from out of which the as-yet uncodified new enters into existence? My argument is that it is not possible to mediate it. But that if we are attentive to it then we can live in a world – and please let us take this term seriously – of adventure. We can also be makers of sounds and images which can create windows upon the chaos.

If we are not attentive to chaos then we are just tourists, gazing at the passing parade of the already encountered, of the already known and pre-packaged, dominated by that order rather than breaking it and re-making it. Desublimated, we consume what it offers us, then we resume being that necessary precondition of the tourist: the obedient worker, who accepts their exploitation as long as the annual leave is guaranteed. But instead of tourism, there *can be* adventure – in the sense of *advenire*, where adventure occurs when something new happens, where there is creation and event.

Perhaps the key concept in the field of academic Media and Cultural Studies is that of mediation. This kind of conceptuali-sation is meant to have an emancipatory effect in studying media texts. The emancipatory story goes like this: "these texts are only mediations, not windows upon reality" and "once we see this then we are more able to immunise ourselves against any ideological effect." However along with this apparently emancipatory notion comes its shadow: the emphasis on mediation as a sort of settling – which goes back to its root idea of a settling of disputes and also indicates its occultation of dissensus, or as we might say in a Mouffian way, a denial of the political. This way of thinking cannot hold if we take Meillassoux's and Castoriadis' ontology seriously. Mediation implies that anterior to any media text there once was *some non-chaotic thing* present. In Media Studies this is also a kind of correlationalist thinking which results in an evisceration of the object[60] and assumption of the non-chaotic; there is assumed to be the given, there is assumed to be stability and reproducibility and an obviousness of meaning. But if the ontologies of chaos are right and what is *is* chaos then none of this is founded and indeed mediation as a concept leads to occultation and denial of the reality of chaos with anti-emancipatory consequences.

So what the media is doing when it claims to *mediate* is a constant covering over of the chaos. What Media Studies is doing through its constant reference to mediation is also a constant covering over of the chaos. Instead of those ways of thinking we should think differently. There is no given meaning – there is only a myth of the given of media meaning; there are only our attempts to give form to the world, to imbue it with meaning where none fundamentally exists.

Of course traditional Media Studies fights on the terrain of meaning; it is fundamentally about the politics of the production of meaning. The concept of "mediation" does emphasise the politics of production of meaning but it also occults an ontological truth. It contributes to the forgetting of the question of the non-meaning of being and unintentionally perpetuates myths of meaning about it. In doing this, it also short-circuits out a potentially much more radical and emancipatory question about responsibility for creating the democratic *polis* out of chaos.

So the point of this chapter has been to prove that what is *is* chaos. I have made this argument in order to sustain and support my critique of the media and dominant strands of Media Studies. If what there is *is* essentially the non-given of chaos then when we talk about "the media" an ontological illusion is both perpetuated and masked, and we will all just continue to write footnotes to this denial of chaos. Instead we can learn how to live with chaos. We can also seriously think about how it may be possible to create what Castoriadis calls "windows upon the chaos" and so contribute to the creation of a properly democratic culture. The next chapter is a discussion of how we can live with ontological chaos and is a necessary preliminary to later considerations of how we may be able to create windows upon the chaos.

Chapter Three

Emancipation after Media

The last chapter contained an argument that what is *is* chaos. This chapter takes the consequences of that argument further and asks how can the thinking of ontological chaos be emancipatory?

How to live with chaos I

First stage: Accept chaos and otherness

If what is *is* chaos in the sense delineated in the last chapter then we will have experiences of the new and of otherness. Castoriadis clarifies what an experience of otherness is like. It can be an experience in our personal lives – the example he gives is the experience of falling in love, the amorous encounter, the *coup de foudre*. Or it can be produced through a particular experience of art – for example when having an experience of one kind of artwork immediately followed by an experience of an artwork which is radically different, perhaps when after viewing a Rembrandt we then view a Twombly. The example he himself gives is literary: the experience of otherness one gets if one reads Kafka's *The Castle* after reading *Madame Bovary*. Or it can be an everyday but paroxystic experience such as "when we look at a rock, and suddenly see a worm moving on the rock." These experiences of otherness testify to the chaos of what is.

> The otherness separating *Gaspard de la nuit* from the *Rasumowsky Quartets* and the latter from *The Art of the Fugue* is not comparable – and the chronological distance between these works (measured in... calendar time) gives us only external benchmarks. Otherness is irreducible, indeducible and not producible.[61]

These advents of otherness can occur every day or any day, and many of us, if not all, have had such experiences. In Castoriadis' thinking this kind of experience is a conduit to autonomy as it forces us to ask: why should I prefer this current way of living and not this other(ness)? Why these rules and laws rather than some others?

Second stage: Be ready for radical reflection
Imagine I had only seen artworks by Rembrandt or similar, then what kind of state of affect am I likely to attain to when I am confronted with, say, a work seemingly just made up of scribbles and scratches such as those produced by Cy Twombly? Even if I am open to this kind of encounter then it is reasonable to suppose that I may start to ask myself many questions about the nature of art, perhaps even about the nature of what is. I could react by refusing this new kind of experience but that would be at a cost – a denial of the experience of colour and form that a Twombly offers. That is, I could refuse the experience of otherness or chaos in which I am suddenly thrown. Alternatively I could depose myself with respect to the chaos I am experiencing. Then arises the question of whether this thing I was calling "I" should stay within its seeming autarky or alter itself to respond to the otherness that has emerged out of the chaos – but which has now been recognised.

How can subjects best exist in this situation of chaos? They would have to have courage, the courage to experience it, acknowledge it, come to terms with it, and live according to the possibility that a very different kind of existence is always possible, and that as a subject you are never at the end of your history – the unknown is always in front of you[62] and in need of reflection.

What kind of reflection? For Castoriadis in reflectiveness we have the possibility that the subject's own activity becomes an "object," the self being explicitly posited as a nonobjective object or as an object that is an object simply by its being posited as such and not by nature... And it is to the extent that one can be for oneself an object by being posited as an object and not by nature that the other, in the true sense of the term, becomes possible... reflection implies the possibility of scission and internal opposition... therefore also the possibility of putting oneself into question.

This is the moment of Rimbaud's "*Je est un autre.*" The life of the subject becomes an object for it – I become an other. The subject is not a natural object but a phenomenon caught as if it were an object in the moment of reflection. Thereby the "naturalness" of the link between a subject and its actions is put into question by the act of reflection. Let me explain further. Every day we act in ways that are more or less habitual, wake up, get out of bed, drag a comb across the head etc. These actions are as if natural. But if I stop and ask what I am doing, if I interrupt this pattern in my life through reflection, and then ask, for example: "How did I get here?" – then the habitual "naturalness" of my actions is annihilated. I stand outside of my state, I am ec-static and this extraordinary moment can cause me to put my actions into question. At this point my activity as subject becomes an object for me and there is the possible realisation that there may be other such kinds of objects, in other words the me-object could be a very different, very other, kind of person.

So a reflection on and a coming to terms with and, in some ways, an acceptance of the chaos are essential for a process of putting instituted individual or social significations into question. The challenge of otherness releases a sense of autonomy – of our responsibility for deciding which laws we wish to adopt in order to govern ourselves.

Third stage: Imagine – See Y in X
If we decide to change the rules that we govern ourselves with, then this calls upon our imaginative capacities – imagination can lead to the creation of ways of thinking about how we should live that are radically different to ones considered at the moment. Linking to my argument in Chapter Two, imagination is another kind of psychic activity characterised by ontological chaos.

> It is because its [the human subject's] imagination is unbridled that it can reflect; otherwise it would be limited to calculating, to "reasoning." Reflectiveness presupposes that it is possible for the imagination to posit as existing that which is not, to see Y in X.

So reasoning would only entail the consideration of existing possible options and thus there is a closure around the possibilities reasoned about. But for Castoriadis imagination is key to the process of radical action:

> One must be able to imagine something other than what is to be able to will; and one must will something other than what is to liberate the imagination... everyday experience constantly shows this: when one does not will anything other than what is, the imagination is inhibited and repressed; in this case, it represents only the eternal perpetuation of what is. And if one cannot imagine something other than what is, every decision is only a choice between possible givens – given by life as it existed beforehand and by the instituted system – which can always be reduced to the results of a calculation or some form of reasoning.

But there is a radical imagination which welcomes the otherness of the other to a point beyond tolerance, to a point where the

overturning of the existing instituted subject and already instituted political options becomes a reality. This is in contrast to
the usual way of thinking politics in such a way as to limit the
political imagination which would have serious consequences
for the political will and ultimately for the creation of social
institutions. The latter leads to a politics of the eternal perpetu-
ation of what is and closure to otherness and so of a kind of
purgatorial political crisis and a kind of deadness. For example
if one only imagines a new form of democracy pretty much
along the lines as envisaged by liberal philosophers in which
one seeks an *ego-alter ego* type dialogue then the resultant
political vision is deadening: a *melange* of already existing
political ideas derived from the dominant social democratic
regimes of the time.

The stream of human creation evident through reflecting
upon the social-historical proves the creative nature of what is.
We are creative. We have imagination which provokes the will
which leads to political action and actual change to newly instituted societies. These can never be entirely ordered or settled
because there is always an anarchic instituting power behind the
social-historical.

Fourth stage: Autonomy

If we had a culture in which the acknowledgement of ontological
chaos was a key characteristic then what would follow in terms
of politics? In order to answer this question we can reflect upon
previous moments in the history of humanity. Which examples
might help us? Castoriadis' answer is the example of Athens of
the ancient Greeks: the culture that produced both democracy
and philosophy, both of which manifested, according to
Castoriadis, out of chaos which played a large part in that
society's imaginary. Why would an imaginary in which chaos
plays such a part lead to the creation of these two phenomena?
The answer is that if there is ontological chaos then anyone who

proposes that we should live together according to immutable laws cannot hold sway. The way we should live together can be determined by us and us alone – no Gods, no Masters, no Laws of History, can tell us. In other words politics in the form of democracy emerges – only the *demos* can rule and yet this rule is always open to question; therefore established laws are always open to question. A similar kind of questioning comes with philosophy: the calling into question of the "truths" instituted by tradition.

> The creation of democracy is philosophically, a response to the a-sensible order of the world, and the exit from hubris. Simultaneously and consubstantially, it contains the recognition that no nature or tradition (or divine prescription) contains the norm which could regulate human affairs. The *polis* sets down and creates its law in contingency, knows it as such, and affirms itself through such acts, since the law, a result of a deliberation, is itself always subject to discussion and possible modification and abrogation.

So the imaginary of chaos engenders both the production of democracy and that of philosophy; the two creations are themselves in a necessary (and historically contingent) relationship. Not one without the other but both determined by the "total indetermination" of chaos. Such is the value of the recognition of ontological chaos. **We live with chaos as autonomous subjects.**

How to live with chaos II

The adventure of the chaotic

With Castoriadis and Meillassoux the connections and echoes are so striking that it really is worth having a close look at the criss-crossing of thoughts and ideas between the two. But that is not all, as I do not just want to present their ideas and their similarities and distinctions, but also to use one against the other in order to open up some new thinking about the relationship between ontological chaos, what happens, and the capacities of human thought.

The new as advent or creation

First I want to explore Meillassoux's account of potentiality and virtuality in order to then go on to try and draw some more radical conclusions from it, and in the spirit of Meillassoux to make substantial claims for the capacity of human thought and action.

What is impressive about Meillassoux is the illuminating attention he gives to long standing philosophical problems. One such is the problem of induction bequeathed to us from David Hume. Meillassoux's proposed solution is via an ontological analysis of a problem that hitherto looked like simply an episte-mological problem and had led to an *aporia*. The problem concerns the fact that we can't know what will happen in the future simply based on what has so far taken place. However taking Meillassoux's analysis it is not a lack of knowledge of Christian festivities that meant that Bertrand Russell's fowl lost his head. It is simply that ontologically speaking, things can just change for no reason because what is *is* hyper-chaos. Meillassoux writes:

> we thus make irruption *ex nihilo* the very concept of a tempo-rality delivered to its pure immanence. Time thus conceived is not governed by any non-temporal principle – it is delivered to the pure immanence of its chaos, its illegality.[63]

There can be events which are not conditioned by potentiality but which, rather, are the children of virtuality, *ex-nihilo* irrup-tions. What examples does Meillassoux give of cases arising from virtuality? Only a few: the advent of life out of dead matter; the surging forth of rational thought. Others are possible for Meillassoux, one possibly being the keystone for some kind of new religious cult (The Church of Radical Contingency?), that being the appearance of a hitherto inexisting divine being. For Meillassoux the advent of life and any such advent would be "an apparition which can only be thought as a supplement irreducible to the conditions of its advent." Why is this?

> I accord to time the capacity to bring forth new laws which were not "potentially" contained in some fixed set of possibles... I accord to time the capacity to bring forth situations which were not at all contained in precedent situations: of creating new cases, rather than merely actualising potentialities that eternally pre-exist their fulguration.

This is why we cannot predict the future based on past events. We have the problem of induction because of the nature of what is – what is is hyper-chaos.

> If we maintain that becoming is not only capable of bringing forth cases on the basis of a pre-given universe of cases, we must then understand that it follows that such cases irrupt, properly speaking, from nothing, since no structure contains them as eternal potentialities before their emergence.

These paroxystic happenings have much in common with Castoriadis' vision of creation out of chaos, *ex-nihilo*. And Meillassoux's *time-as-creation* and Castoriadis' *being-as-creation* also have their striking similarities. However whereas for Meillassoux an advent is extremely rare, it seems (at least from reading *After Finitude*), for Castoriadis we are essentially creation – what is *is* creation. Hence something so constant and everyday – not to say every moment – such as when we see colour is an act of creation, and otherness is likely to irrupt at any moment as for example when we see Castoriadis' worm begin to move out of the hitherto presumed dead matter.

When juxtaposing these two strands of philosophical thinking – that of Meillassoux and that of Castoriadis – questions start to spring up. For example, why doesn't Meillassoux use the term creation? Why are advents so rare? There is a lot of talk of bringing forth and of the creating of virtuality but why so little room for an artwork or a logical argument – creations – to be counted themselves as something like advent-creations? Why not produce, so to speak, micro-advents? Why emphasise time as the force of change and not in some sense a subject? Isn't there a difference in nature between the advent of life – a fundamentally biological thing – and the advent of rational thought? If the initial commencement of rational thought is an advent, then why is not every rational thought an advent? What makes my next logical thought so different from the first ever logical thought? Rational thought does not just reproduce itself, subjectlessly. We could instead argue that rational thought may not be the cause of itself but rather arise from a micro change in the laws of what is. So then each time a rational thought would be a creation – anarchic time surging through a subject. What is an artwork if not an example of this surging forth? A thought, every thought would then be an act of creation or an advent to use Meillassoux's term.

We can read Meillassoux's book on Mallarmé, partly against him and as in part a supplement to *After Finitude*. When Mallarmé says every throw of the dice emits a thought, a throw of a dice is to be understood as a manifestation of ontological chaos, as is the thought that it emits. So every logical thought that occurs can be considered to be an advent. I propose, by merging Mallarmé with Meillassoux, that every logical thought is the result of an ontological throw of the dice – so that we can think of every thought as advent.[64]

Meillassoux emphasises hyper-chaos as the harbinger of the

possible collapse of everything. We could rethink it, perhaps no less terrifyingly, as the creator of new forms – and it could be an emancipatory role of image and sound workers to capture these new forms.

Chapter Four

How to Live: The Existential Subject

Meillassoux is often described as having a mentor and that mentor is Alain Badiou. His philosophy has been thoroughly analysed and exegised over the last few years and so I do not want to spend time doing it again here. But briefly Badiou is concerned with how the new can enter the world and he calls this moment of the new an "event." However two important issues arise once we consider the philosophies of the event and creation as set out by Castoriadis and Badiou:

1. The issue of the new and how to respond to it. In what follows I will frame my argument in terms of the following question: Should we be like Socrates or Saint Paul?
2. The issue of how often an event (Badiou) or an advent (Meillassoux) or a creation (Castoriadis) takes place.

For Badiou the inconsistent multiplicity of *what is* is crucial and he is able to furnish a theory to account for it; with Castoriadis there is a posited chaos, the support for which is based on the continually changing products of human history as well as everyday experiences of otherness. Both affirm the new and I argue the new is necessarily anarchic, in this precise sense: the advent of the new is anarchic because it provides the potential for reconsideration of what we take to be the state of things, that which has the authority of being taken for granted, the "way things are." The new is a challenge to those already in authority; it potentially can create a critical relationship to the accepted, the traditional and the dominant.

The subject in Badiou and Castoriadis

Badiou's subject is convoked by the event and has meaningful existence only as a result of events. Castoriadis' subject is a creator of forms. This is where they especially differ. And it is here that serious doubts arise about Badiou's thought and the politics that flow from it. This difference between the two philosophers could be encapsulated in the tale of two different types of subject: Saint Paul and Socrates.

Against Saint Paul

Badiou is an atheist but one who has written a book admiring the way Paul behaved after his experience of an event on the road to Damascus. Here we have the Badiouian subject as a witness.[65] The witness has a long history in theological debate and experience and has even been a key part in sectarian Christian movements; one well-known sect is called precisely Jehovah's Witnesses. Yet quite astonishingly here we have a post-Marxist thinker once more invoking this figure of the witness. And although he couches his discourse of political activity in the dry language of set theory, another way of considering his idea of political activity is in terms of the inspired evangelical, a sectarian figure.

Perhaps even more disconcerting is Badiou's statement that even though subjects do not understand events nevertheless they should be true to them, but isn't this antithetical to egalitarian political organisation, not to say the philosophical enterprise itself? Elsewhere Badiou's advice to militants is simply *"continuez"* or "carry on." Surely we should ask why continue? Surely we are entitled to reason? What space is there for our critical faculties here? So for me, the problem with Badiou is the problem of the faithful subject which may entail a possible conse-quent negation of autonomy.

For Saint Paul

On the other hand, perhaps there are good reasons for the affirmation of the event. Why should we be faithful to a Badiouian event? Because as we find it very difficult to grasp the new, we risk missing the experience of something that can turn our world around, "we hear new music badly." In *Beyond Good and Evil,* Nietzsche states:

> With a given stimulus, our eye finds it more comfortable to produce once more an image that has already been produced frequently than to capture something different and new in an impression. To do the latter requires more power, more "morality." To listen to something new is embarrassing and hard on our ears; we hear strange music badly. When we hear some different language, we spontaneously try to reshape the sounds we hear into words which sound more familiar and native to us.

> Something new finds our senses hostile and reluctant, and in general, even with the "simplest" perceptual processes, the emotions like fear, love, hate, including the passive feeling of idleness, *are in control.*[66]

So we hear new and strange music badly, yet we know that new music can turn out to be astounding and important music. So how can we experience the new well? Think about the first time one has an experience of abstract art – the first Pollock, or the Cy Twombly mentioned earlier. Or the first time you hear almost any musical piece by Ligeti or even Beethoven's *Das Grosse Fuge,* or The Pop Group's *Y* album. Or the first time you attend a properly democratic political demonstration. Or are taken by a philosophical idea? Or don't "get" some poetry (but still feel somehow drawn to it)? It can all seem just too strange; we do experience newness badly. But we can later come to cherish these things. What happens in between these two states? What is needed to see value in the new? How much is an affirmation akin to a leap of faith and how important is the exercise of autonomy in the face of such an event?

Why do we begin thinking politically? Deleuze states that:

Something in the world forces us to think. This something is an object not of recognition but a fundamental "encounter." What is encountered may be Socrates, a temple or a demon. It may be grasped in a range of affective tones: wonder, love, hatred, suffering. In whichever tone, its primary characteristic is that it can only be sensed. In this sense it is opposed to recognition.[67]

This may be an experience of injustice or an experience of disappointment.[68] Anyway there is a not-yet-fully cognised event and we start to think about change and therefore to think politically.

The great appeal of Badiou's thought is the focus on the encounter and on the notion of the event, and its force as truth-creating, where truth is considered as something that breaks with accepted doxa and ideology or accepted opinion, the kind of truth that human history has shown us to be extremely valuable. His thinking creates a kind of Nietzschean doubt about the habits of human cognition – could the so-called rational human subject with its critical faculties intact simply smother the significance of events and ideas through a kind of propositional interrogation and so lay festering in its own accepted habitual patterns of understanding?

It may be more than anecdotally interesting to consider what happens when Badiou and Castoriadis begin to create some kind of political body. With Badiou the obscurity of the event is matched by the obscurity of the name of his militant grouping (one that had very few other members, he admits) simply known as *The Political Organisation*. With Castoriadis we get the declarative nature of his theoretical-political group *Socialism or Barbarism* and the grounded nature of his acceptance that human history is made up of creations, some incontestably despicable – the Gulag, the Holocaust – and some valuable – socialism, the works of JS Bach, and his emphasis upon the evident being of the social-historical. One organisation is rather obscure; the other is much clearer and more open.

There is an impasse. The impasse being that on the one hand we should strive for autonomy and on the other hand we should be open to the new. This is a difficult place to be. Saying yes to an event without thinking about it or knowing why we should affirm it often seems to be too much of a sacrifice. However which of us knows infallibly what will be the consequences of our actions? None of us, and that is the reality of courage, the proof that it exists, so we must admit that we do often say yes to something without knowing all of the consequences of that affirmation. Without such uncertainty courage could not exist. Think of the courage of those who volunteered to fight for the left against the fascists in the Spanish Civil War, or the Parisian communards – those who have left historical examples of courage for us to consider today. Or the lovers who affirm the amorous event but who suffer. (Is there any lover who does not suffer?)

At this point I want to borrow a notion from Rancière's writings about images and rework it. The notion of the pensive, in Rancière's work, specifically addresses this moment of uncertainty. He writes of the moment when there is something in an image which is somehow resistant to thought – "the act of thinking seems to be encroached upon by a certain passivity."[69] The adventure of thinking I would like to commence here is to transpose Rancière's term "image" and substitute for it the term "event." The existential image/event is the one which contains an "unthought thought" as if the image/event has no clarity as per an intention or a purpose but yet has an effect on the person who experiences it. "Pensiveness thus refers to a condition that is indeterminately between the active and the passive." And Rancière adds that this is also an indeterminacy between thought and non-thought.

For Castoriadian thought this is a chaotic moment, recalling for now Castoriadis' definition of the chaotic or chaos as that of radical indeterminacy, it is also therefore an an-archic moment as no authority can hold in the face of this indeterminacy. Castoriadis' thought leaps at this point to the assumption that at such an impasse we will assume our responsibility and create our own *nomos* as a way of responding to the event. We can either attain autonomy or stay mired in heteronomy. But between the two, I suggest, there is something else. Autonomy itself is risk, affirmation, existential choice. But revisability is also built into it. That's what makes autonomy more radically anti-foundational than either Badiou's neo-Platonism or Meillassoux's neo-Cartesianism.

Perhaps we should follow Rancière when he says that pensiveness can be designated as a "tangle between several forms of indeterminacy."[70] For Rancière pensiveness arises when you have the impossibility of making two "images" coincide. Here we could suggest that our dilemma is one where the two responses to an event cannot coincide. That is the moment when the response of autonomy and the response of affirmation of the event without knowing why we should affirm it, cannot coincide. So we are in a state of pensiveness. What could then happen is not a choice of one or the other but their conjunction. Rancière discusses the tension between "identity" (which here could correspond to the notion of autonomy) and "raw presences" (which here could correspond to events) – where pensiveness conjoins two regimes of expression without homogenising them. This may be the kind of understanding we are looking for, one that maintains a focus on the thinking of the unthought and yet is also able to maintain the value of autonomy. This is what I would like to call the moment of the existential subject. Why is this existential? Because it is a moment without any fallback on essentialist notions of identity, we are just in the midst of a kind of existential tension in which we have to think critically. And because it looks to the future and sees the possibility of the new, the unthought, yet it also places an emphasis on the subject themselves to make a decision using whatever resources are at their disposal, and states that those resources (reason, history, experience, *phronesis*) are all that anyone would have at the moment of decision. That anyone is the democratic-existential subject deplored by Plato.

Chapter Five

Democracy and Media

What could living life as an existential subject have to do with democracy? In order to understand the answer to that question we need to properly understand what is democracy and what is anarchy. But do we even know the meaning of democracy? And do we understand the relationship between democracy and anarchy?[71]

Democracy and anarchy

Democracy is one of those terms that saturates our everyday political talk and especially media talk, and yet all that can produce a soporific acceptance of an illusion. Primarily the illusion that because the media constantly use this word then they *must* know what democracy means. Most media people seem to think that democracy is a state form so that it cannot have anything to do with anarchy, which is anti-authoritarian. But they may not know what democracy (or indeed anarchy) mean – so to start off I want to ask questions about these terms so that we can properly revisit the question of the meaning of democracy.[72] Terms like "democracy" and "anarchy" are abused every day by writers and politicians of all types. For example even the worst dictator will nominate their state as "democratic." Recall the "people's democracies" of such and such a nation, where the nation is so-titled in an attempt to hide the repressive nature of everyday life. Recently Badiou has referred to democracy as the political fetish of *our* time.[73] Similarly "anarchy" is used as a kind of Hobbesian threat: the terrible consequence of questioning authority will be that life will, as a result, be nasty, brutish and short. I want to contest such appropriations so this chapter will entail a political reappropriation of

43

the terms democracy and anarchy.

For me, helpfully, Daniel Colson's recent comprehensive guide to anarchy gives us a definition of it as a:

foundational notion of the libertarian movement, which through time has lost its provocative sense... and has been transformed little by little into "anarchism," a body of ideas and of organisations often antipodean to what the term anarchy signified in the first place in the writings of Déjacque, Coeuderoy, Proudhon, Bakunin etc. Contrary to what is often believed, anarchy isn't reducible to a political utopian model which is forever postponed until the end of time: the absence of government.[74]

Colson goes on to support the idea of an-*archy* referring to the Greek derivation of the word anarchy as "an-*archie*," where *archie* is any sort of authority. So, Colson says:

anarchy is firstly the refusal of all first principles, of all first causes, of all primary ideas, of all dependence of beings on one unique origin.

In order to avoid mistaking anarchy for the antipodean ideologies of anarchism that Colson deplores, I will foreground his notion of anarchy. So, for example, when we think of anarchy we would think of it in terms of no first principles of the superiority of the "learned" over the "ignorant"; or of the rich over the poor; or of the old over the young; or of a foundational original first cause. Rather we would have the recognition of Castoriadian creative chaos or Meillassouxian hyper-chaos. So at this point then Colson's definition of anarchy intersects with the ontological work of Chapter Three. Building on Colson's definition I will argue that conceptualisations of anarchy, after all, amount to a political philosophy of chaos. Furthermore anarchy as the philosophical conceptualisation of chaos is also joined to the notion of democracy as the political acknowledgement of the reality of chaos. To explain exactly how these terms are related is a key project of this chapter.

My conclusion is that democracy is anarchic, insurgent and existential. Here's why.

Initially I will rely upon Josiah Ober's work on the meaning of democracy.[75] Ober's work emphasises that to think of democracy as fundamentally about voting is wrong – as Rousseau pointed out some time ago. Indeed for Ober, "reducing democracy to a voting rule arguably elides much of the value and potential of democracy." I will use Ober's work to clarify the meanings of democracy and anarchy – political-philosophical terms that originated in ancient Greece but, as I have emphasised, have undergone an obscuring of their meaning.

Ober investigates the use of "political types" in ancient Greece and comes to certain interesting conclusions for anyone wanting to clarify the relationship between anarchy and democracy (and I rely heavily on Ober in what follows). Greek terms for political systems tend to utilise the *arche* postfix (meaning authority) – for example in *monarchia* or *oligarchia*, where monarchia is the authority of the one and oligarchia is the authority of the few – but *demokratia* is obviously very different to this. This word does not use the *arche* postfix but rather the terminology of *kratos* – meaning power – and so *demo-kratie* means "people power." What is very interesting is that we can have *demo-kratie* but there is no such thing as *dem-archy*. This fact is one that Ober takes very seriously and with some illuminating exposition leads us to a ground where the troublesome and contested relationship between anarchy and democracy can be clarified. Ober reveals the affinity between democracy and anarchy as he shows that democracy is not a state based electoral procedure based on the numbers of people voting for their preferences:

First, unlike *monarchia* (from the adjective *monos*: solitary) and *oligarchia* (from *hoi oligoi*: the few), *demokratia* is not in the first instance concerned with "number."

So *demokratia* was not about adding up majorities and minorities; it would not make sense to transpose onto it the meaning of democracy that we tend to when we talk about representative democracy which is fundamentally about electoral voting systems. Ober comes to the conclusion that *arche* and *kratos* are about different sorts of power:

> it is reasonable to suppose that *kratos* meant something rather different from *arche* and pointed to a different conception of power.

There is no conjunction of meaning between *an-arche* and *a-kratos*. *Arche* is about number but *kratos* is not. The well-known Greek term for those unable to control themselves is *akrasia* – literally without the power to do something. So if *kratos* is not about numbers and voting then what is it about?

> *kratos*, when it is used as a regime-type suffix, becomes power in the sense of strength, enablement, or "capacity to do things."

Importantly then Ober goes on to suggest that democracy is not about gaining control of some kind of state-based body or as he puts it "constitutional apparatus."

In sum, rather than imagining the *-kratos* group as sharing the *-arche* group's primary concern for the control of a (pre-existing) constitutional apparatus, Ober's work would suggest that the *-kratos*-root terms originally referred to a (newly) activated political capacity.

So democracy as demokratia means, more broadly, something like the power of the demos "to effect change in the public

realm." It is not about the reflection of preset political preferences but rather it is about the surging up of a popular political
capacity – so democracy, at least as *demokratia*, is insurgent. This
notion of insurgent democracy does of course sound strange to
the ears of those who can only think of democracy as "representative." When those people link representative with a certain sort
of passive democracy Ober concludes that:

> they are placing democracy on a par with oligarchy, as little
> more, in principle or practice, than the monopoly over estab-
> lished governmental offices by, respectively, the many (poor)
> and the few (wealthy), is to accept fifth-century anti-democ-
> ratic polemics as an accurate description of political reality.

This book does not accept this oligarchical interpretation of its
enemy democracy. It reclaims the affinity between philosophy
and democracy because indeed philosophy does itself have some
affinity with this insurgent phenomenon of democracy –
philosophy itself is insurgent in the sense that it surges up and
challenges what are the commonly held assumptions of the day.
These themes of democracy as insurgent and democracy as being
not at all a state form have been insightfully conceptualised by
Miguel Abensour, Jacques Rancière and Jean-Luc Nancy. It is
their work that I want to use in order to develop my argument
that democracy will be anarchic or not at all. Abensour's work
helps us to understand how democracy is insurgent and
Rancière's work helps us understand the anarchical nature of
democracy. Finally Nancy's comments on democracy and human
nature point toward a conceptualisation of democracy as the
existential-political.

Miguel Abensour sketches the form of a dissensual
democracy which he calls insurgent democracy. This is not a
surging up of democracy within the commonly accepted field of
the political as defined in the terms of the liberal democratic

47

state. Instead Abensour conceptualises democracy as situating itself outside of that field; democracy, for him, is against the state:

> Insurgent democracy is not a variant of conflictual democracy, but its exact opposite. Whereas conflictual democracy practices conflict in the interior of the state, of the democratic state, which in its very name, gives itself away as an avoidance of the primary conflict, inclining conflictuality at the same time towards permanent compromise, but insurgent democracy situates conflict in another place, exterior to the state, against it, and well away from the avoidance of the major conflict: democracy against the state.[76]

This is because true democracy follows an anarchical impulse against the principle of authority, and as the key institution in liberal democracy which embodies authority is the state, this is democracy against the state:

> Insurgent democracy is born from the intuition that there is no true democracy without reactivating the profound impulse of democracy against all forms of *arche*, an anarchic impulse which stands therefore as first priority against the classic manifestation of the *arche* – namely, the state.[77]

In much political philosophy there is an impulse to replace the political with the social but with Abensour we can see an alternative vision of democracy which embraces interminable political conflict against the state.

> In place of conceiving emancipation as the victory of the social (a reconciled civil society) over politics, at the same time leading to the disappearance of politics, this form of democracy makes appear, works towards the permanent appearance of, a political community against the state. In

place of the opposition of the social and the political, it substitutes that of the political and the state.[78]

At this point another political relationship opens up: the state is knocked off its throne, and instead of seeing the state and democracy as natural bedfellows, this relationship is denaturalised:

Dethroning the state, it puts politics against the state and reopens the abyss too often hidden between politics and the state.[79]

And once the hidden is once more clearly visible it becomes more evident that democracy is anti-state or it isn't at all, and that:

Democracy is the theatre of a permanent insurrection against the state, against all forms of state, the unificationist, the integrationist, the organising state.[80]

Although Abensour's thoughts are rich and provocative they do need support from a conceptualisation of democracy which more clearly argues out the links between anarchy and democracy. Jacques Rancière's work on the nature of politics does just that.

There are a couple moves to be made to make the case that democracy is anarchic as well as insurgent. Firstly we need to say what an *arkhè* is. Secondly we then need to see why democracy is without *arkhè* – so by definition anarchic.

What is an *arkhè*? Rancière refers us back to Plato to understand this notion of *arkhè*. Plato sets out six situations when one group is apparently qualified to rule over another: when the old rule over the young, when parents rule over children, when the master rules over the slave, when nobles rule over villains, when the strong rule over the weak and when the learned rule over the ignorant. An *arkhè* is established when there is a clear distribution of roles e.g. that between a parent and a child, or a clear set of capacities that establish superiority of one group over another such as that of the apparently learned over the apparently ignorant. However Plato also discusses a seventh situation which some may claim in some way legitimates rule. This he calls the "drawing of lots" – that is, democracy. But what is peculiar is that democracy does not meet the usual criteria for legitimate rule; it is neither a pre-determined distribution of roles nor an apparent capacity for ruling. "The 'drawing of lots' presents the paradox of a 'qualification without qualification,' of one that spells the absence of arkhè."[81] So Rancière concludes:

> Democracy means precisely that the "power of the demos" is the power of those that no arkhè entitles them to... It is an anarchic principle that must be presupposed for politics to exist at all and in so far as it is anarchic it precludes the self-grounding of politics.

Where there are politics there is the questioning and revolt against rule; it is the moment of the recognition that there is no real reason why someone should rule over another. This questioning, the opening up of a chasm, the attack on the foundational, the acknowledgement of chaos, this is the moment of democracy and of anarchy. It is the acknowledgement that the *kratie* of the *demos* is without an entitlement to rule, it is without *arkhè* – so democracy is the politics of the an-*arkhè*. Democracy is anarchic as it acknowledges the chasmic.

As Nancy emphasises:

> The point is that the word democracy seems to contain an internal barrier to the possibility of a foundational principle. Indeed, I would go so far as to say that democracy essentially implies an element of anarchy... the right or law the democratic institution generates has no real existence other than its own unceasing and active relationship to its own lack of foundation.[82]

Nancy then interestingly links democracy as political entity to an anti-essentialist politics:

> not only is there no such thing as "human nature," but "humankind" homme is virtually incommensurable with anything you could call a "nature"... (it) far outstrips anything we could call "natural."

And then Nancy comes to the following conclusion that, in my interpretation, links democracy to the existential:

> Democracy, as a species to the genus politics, is incapable of being grounded in a transcendent principle. So the only thing that grounds or founds democracy is an absence: the absence of any human nature.

There are lots of echos of Sartrian existentialism here. Democracy is existential because it cannot be founded in a political or more ultimately a human nature. It cannot be founded in an authoritative conception of what it means to be human; there is no democratic essence rooted in a human nature. We are free and in our freedom, we are condemned to be democratic. All other attempts to legitimate the exercise of political power are lies, fabricated by *des salauds*, acts of *mauvaise foi*. So democracy is anarchic, existential and insurgent.

Using these conceptualisations which allow us to see that democracy is anarchic and insurgent and existential, we can now consider how well the media is able to deal with this chaotic phenomenon of democracy. The exact opposite of these qualities underlies the following exchange heard on BBC Radio 4 where a *salaud* is described as a democrat even though he will not allow kissing in public, and the reason he is being discussed at all is because he is anti-insurgent and authoritarian. The discussion is about Turkish leader Erdogan. This is how the BBC, in this instance, promulgates authoritarianism as democracy.

Here is a snippet from a conversation from the BBC's flagship *Today* news programme. The anchorman John Humphreys and correspondent Chris Morris are discussing 2013's dissent in Turkey on 12 June 2013. Their discussion started around 7.09, on Erdogan the Turkish Prime Minister:

Morris: The economy... has been democratised by Erdogan, but he has never shaken off a disregard for the freedom to dissent, the freedom to be different from him.
Humphreys: So he is an authoritarian... er... he is a democrat, but he is, if there is such a thing, an authoritarian democrat.

As Frank Webster[83] points out, the BBC is a parliamentary creation and has been profoundly affected in its assumptions by the parliamentary model which created it and so it is highly unlikely to, in its normal mode of functioning, recognise democracy as a non-state phenomenon. It seems in this case a key journalist working for it articulates democracy to a form of authoritarian fascism. This restricted view of democracy was pretty obvious right from the beginning when Reith, at the time of the UK General Strike of 1926, and in his role as the first Director General of the BBC, declared that the state government was itself democratic ("for the people") and so the state-created BBC was for the state government: "Assuming that the BBC is for the people, and that the Government is for the people, it follows that the BBC must be for the government in this crisis too."

The scandal of democracy

Rancière uses the term "the scandal of democracy" to expose the fact there is no legitimation for a so-called politics of governance. The furore around Russell Brand's appearance on the BBC's *Newsnight* is just such a democratic scandal and it shows the problem with mediating anarchic democracy. Brand is interviewed by veteran Jeremy Paxman, well-known for his abrasive interviewing style, although he suspends that here perhaps signaling to the audience that we should not be taking Brand too seriously. Russell Brand is a working-class public figure and comedian, who has ended up being rather rich. This in itself has caused trouble. It is an identity that can't be easily assigned into a role. The Brand identity vacillates – it is disordered and it causes disorder. It is already an-archic because as Rancière suggests for an *arkhè* to exist there needs to be a clear set of designated roles – one has to be either one of the ruled or one of the rulers. So in relation to this disordered identity what is quite revealing is that Paxman's first question begins, "Russell Brand, who are you...?" There is an attempt to assign that role from the off. It is also to suggest that as a member of the demos, just like Darcus Howe, Brand has no right to speak. Brand's reply again refuses the assignation of role and the acceptance of criteria for being in that role (in this case the editor of a political magazine, for one week – the UK's *New Statesman*). Paxman asks Brand if he participates in the oligarchy reproducing, begrudgingly, the democratic practice of voting, Brand famously replies that he doesn't, and Paxman then suggests that Brand can have no authority to think about politics, not realising that this kind of active nihilism is a moment of the refusal of *arkhè*, so it can itself be democratic, and is most certainly a political moment, when the acceptance of the role of rulers and ruled is called into question and politics emerges.[84]

The question then comes about of how one group may acquire political power. Paxman surely somewhat naively suggests that power is bestowed upon "people" by them being voted in. A classic liberal occultation of the true bases of power in Western capitalist societies. This is being baldly stated even after the Occupy movement has highlighted the gross disparities in power and wealth, their argument is one that Paxman has either not acknowledged or implicitly dismissed. "In a democracy that's how it works," interjects Paxman – again, just as with the example of Darcus Howe, the interview starts to be cacophonous and abusive just at this point when the nature of democracy itself is under question – "why should we listen to you when you can't be arsed to vote?" Paxman demands. Thereby legitimating, or trying to legitimate, his own political authority as one of those who presides over the legitimacy of those we vote for. By such a statement Paxman is effectively attempting to close down the meaning of democracy and politics anchoring it to the limits of a voting procedure and suggesting that we can change things only by voting.[85] Paxman finally asserts that Brand does not believe in democracy as he wants a revolution – as if revolution could not be a democratic moment – when of course history shows plenty of democratic revolutionary moments. So it is strange to think that Paxman is a product of the elite public school/Oxbridge British education system when he is capable of such ignorance.

Or perhaps it is not so strange. The BBC is part of the system of governance of the UK. It, as well as parliament and the cabinet, is staffed by members of the elite classes who have assumed a model of governance by expertise. The assumptions of the experts are the right ones and indubitable – it is what Rancière would call a "government of science" which

will always end up a government of "natural elites," in which the social power of those with expert competences is combined with the power of wealth, at the cost once more of provoking a democratic disorder that displaces the boundaries of the political.[86]

Which is exactly what the Brand interview does. It is a moment of democratic disorder akin to the moment when the indignants in Athens lasered the established media. So democracy has a deep affiliation with disorder and chaos. It represents a moment when a people acknowledge chaos and the non-foundation of politics. But we must also acknowledge that it requires an existential subjectivity to sustain it, and the actions that follow from sustaining that subjectivity are courageous actions. Democracy is claimed and reclaimed by what Rancière calls "singular and precarious acts"; these are actions committed in chaos without the safety nets of any *arkhè*.

It follows that when George Steiner asked rhetorically, "Does democracy know how to encourage this act of rebellion, of interior revolt which is at the heart of great literature and art?"[87] as if it never could, he was wrong... Contra-Steiner the answer would be yes, because democracy is the political acknowledgement of ontological chaos under which, for example, the ancient Greeks created tragedy. So the existential democratic subject would have to be attuned to the new, that which surges up, that which is insurgent, that which arises out of the chasmic society – the chaos. It would also be existential in that the moment of democratic choice would be inevitable and inescapable and recognised as such; to that extent Steiner's comments are a manifestation of political bad faith.

Some would say that we belong to certain societies and that we should accept the norms that these societies produce, even including among those norms the dominant way of conceiving democracy. We should rather think beyond the moment in time, by thinking of ourselves across and through time and not just "in" particular moments of time. This would be a kind of radical existential thinking. The usual mode of thinking democracy stops well short of recommending the kind of society which is capable of living the never-ending process of autonomy, of putting its institutions and laws into question, of giving itself its own laws. Rather that usual way of thinking lives in fear of the mortality of its own ways of making sense of the world; it is the institutional thinking of those who live in fear of cultural death and shy away from a radical embrace of autonomy. Here we start to glimpse the kind of existential democracy which will be fallible, mortal, aware of its limitations and of the value of the unknown. We are starting to realise that it is not possible to live democratically without embracing, with René Char, the unknown in front of us. It is in recognition of such chaos that we must begin the adventure of existential democracy.

Chapter Six

Windows upon the Chaos

How can it be possible for makers of images and sounds to create a window upon the chaos?[88]

Castoriadis emphasises that artworks cannot mediate chaos because it is "beyond or beneath all signification," but windows upon the chaos may be able to show the sense of the a-sensible and a-sensibility of sense.[89] In order to explain further Castoriadis discusses Shakespeare's *King Lear*. The reader may be familiar with this tragedy. The old king is trying to find a *sensible* way to pass on the power and the kingdom to his three daughters. He summons them and in their conversations with him the first two daughters express a *meaning* for human life – it is about love for one another and especially about the love of parents for their children and of the children for their parents. So the enchanted Lear decides that the *sensible* way to divide the kingdom is in three – between the three daughters. But the last of the three, Cordelia, sees the doubled meaning of the speeches of the two sisters: apparently filial but really inspired by commercial interests. She cannot bring herself to make the same kind of enchanting speech and simply says she loves the King as his daughter and nothing else. Lear, in some sense *sensibly*, reacts badly. He excludes Cordelia from the sharing of the kingdom. So, for Castoriadis, in this play, things begin to unfold in a way which is both comprehensible, meaningful, *sensible* but also at the same time atrocious and completely *non-sensible*. Everybody will be destroyed in this affair through acts that are completely understandable – given the life of passion that is the life of humans – and *a-sensible*. All the actors have their reasons and meanings for their actions but all of those reasons and meanings die with them ending up at an *a-sensible* totality. Such is the *sense of the a-sensible* and the *a-sensibility of sense.*

The generic aspect here is also important, Castoriadis argues that tragedy has a special ability to act as a window upon the chaos:

> What tragedy... gives us all to see, is that Being is Chaos. Chaos is exhibited here, first, as the absence of order for man, the lack of positive correspondence between human intentions and actions, on the one hand, and their result or outcome on the other. More than that tragedy shows that not only are we not masters of the consequences of our actions, but that we are not even masters of their meaning. Chaos is also presented as Chaos in man, that is as his hubris.

Through King Lear we have a window upon the chaos; we, for Castoriadis, get a glimpse of the *a-sensibility* of sense. He also names other artworks that also open up windows upon the chaos, mentioning musical works by Bach and Mozart, and Wagner's *Tristan und Isolde; Ulysses* by Joyce, and other literary works by Balzac, Kafka and Flaubert.

> They condense art as a window upon the abyss, upon chaos and they give form to this abyss – that is the moment of meaning, that's to say the creation by art of a cosmos.

The example of King Lear is one which is interpreted as a window upon the chaos by linking together the genre, narrative events and the dialogue's play with the notion of nothingness – "nothing can come of nothing" etc. But I want to propose that we also have examples of audio-visual works that can act as windows upon the chaos. As far as I am aware Castoriadis does not make any references to works of cinema as being valuable works in themselves, and is highly unlikely to discuss popular cinematic works. This must be partly down to his negative evaluation of most artwork produced in the later part of the twentieth century as, for him, part of a generalised cultural and political insignificance. However the notion of artworks – and perhaps we could extend the field to include just some audio-visual works – as windows onto or upon the chaos is useful. But as so far discussed in this book the chaotic can manifest itself in many ways, not just as the *a-sensibility* of sense. We could also see through a window upon the chaos in other ways. In what follows I will give examples of how this is possible, by subversion of genre, by experiencing the chaos of light, by showing filmic advents, by laying bare the non-sense of the seemingly meaningful narrative sense, by showing paroxysms, by clashing together the truth of the image and the truth of the narrative, or by experiencing the intolerable chaos of the cinematic object.

I. Show the abyss, the chasm, the chaos, the a-sensibility of sense through the subversion of generic sense, through the voiding of the expectations and assumptions of the generic

Pan's Labyrinth (Guillermo del Toro) shows us the generic abyss. Critics were often mystified and unable to explain the dual-genre nature of the film. The film clashes together two main generic repertoires – the fantasy film and the war film. The key players in the two generic strands (although which are which?) are a fascist Capitaine and a young girl, Ofelia. Both construct a sense and meaning for themselves in the midst of a political-social chaos at the end of the Spanish Civil War. These meaningful worlds are presented to us, the viewers, as generic. What the film exposes is that the fantasies of the girl – she inhabits a world of magical beings, gods, fairies, monsters etc – are echoed by the fascist fantasies of the Capitaine: fatherland, glory in battle, violence, patriarchy etc. Both come to "nothing" and just as in *Lear,* by the end of the film, the key characters are all dead – the Capitaine, Ofelia and Ofelia's mother. Genre is a mode of sense-making, a way of containing and exploring a sometimes very closed, sometimes quite open repertoire of images and sounds. What the film shows us is the *a-sensibility* of genre sense.

2. Show the chaos of the material you are working within – the chaos of light

I have mentioned filmwork by film directors Ben Rivers and Carlos Reygadas as well as artist Hilary Lloyd already in this book. One aspect that all three share is the attention to light in their work. Watching Rivers' *Two Years At Sea* the viewer cannot avoid considering the way the film material and light have interacted. Often pools of white light bloom and flash across the images which themselves have a grainy otherworldly feel to them. In Reygadas' *Silent Light* set in a Mennonite community in Mexico, there are several astonishing moments when light itself erupts onto the screen in high contrast to the daily detail of the ordinarily puritanical key characters' lives. In one such moment two adulterous lovers kiss and as they do circles and ovoids of orange and pink light flare up, and spin and float around them. We are reminded of the chaotic nature of the luminous material of the image.

Hilary Lloyd's artworks are also to a large extent about the appearance and disappearance of light-based objects. We can't help but begin to ask ourselves questions as we experience the art. This stuff – what am I to make of it? Ordinarily it may be that the certainty of objects underlines my own subjective certainty. But with Lloyd's work these are things that appear to be on the edge of the visible and the invisible and so provoke a kind of ontological uncertainty. With this art some alarm registers, yet I want to look, to see, to be here, in front of it. Lloyd's work can have an almost mannered anti-media professionalism about it. It is more or less guaranteed that the techno-code-obsessed editors and pixel-peeping camera operators of the media industries would judge some of the framing and the camera movements to be amateur, with their sudden jolts and movements. But the point is that the camera has caught something – look! We can enter into a proper engagement with Lloyd's work by emphasising the Rancièrian idea of the pensive image and his political thought, which anyway is never separated from his aesthetic thinking. His is thinking of the an-archic, and the consonant anarchic tendency in both Lloyd's personal presence and art would seem a reasonable point for entry into discussion of it.

How might the artwork be pensive and an-archic? Rancière's idea of the pensive image is of an image that conjoins two regimes of expression without homogenising them – so to paraphrase Rancière, Lloyd's work is an art poised between cinema, documentary photography, sculpture and painting, in which none of these regimes dominate – there is an an-archic relationship between them. *Floor* (2011), for instance, has a cinematic projection of light across a space. There is something of documentation – there is clearly an existent object but it is hard to define; it is also beautifully and seemingly haphazardly vertically lined by a purple stripe of light vacillating between appearance and disappearance. Yet, other images in her Turner Prize-nominated collection hardly move and have something of the photograph about them. We sometimes are not sure where to look – indeed *Moon* frustrates our attempts to see both its screens at the same time. The projectors have sculptural qualities. These are also screens which have a long-held affinity with television. So in the artwork there is a Rancièrean refusal of regime domination and there is "resistance to thought" but also because of that a "reawakening of perceptual possibilities." And in interviews Lloyd is "punky" – resistant to thought that may enclose her work within a single regime of expression because the art may, should, must, open up possibilities.

At the very least it is a reminder that the boundaries between the perceivable and the unperceivable can be changed, opened, unpoliced. So this suggests another way of seeing and another way of being, and of course that necessitates thought about other ways of living: politics.

3. Show the chaos of advent

The slow purposeful build of detail, of the mundane and quotidian. There is some drama, a love affair in a very puritanical community. Diegetic sound only throughout, producing the feeling that this is just reality somehow caught on film. A woman breaks down in emotion. She dies. The funeral. An almost documentary-like recording of the community habits. Various characters visit the body as it lies in repose; all this is recorded in slow, somewhat painstaking detail, we have to be patient. A lot of silence. A kiss between the dead wife and her husband's lover. A tear emerges from the closed eyes of the hitherto dead body and slides down the cheek. The eyes begin to flutter, her mouth opens. She speaks. This is the moment of the advent. In Reygadas' *Silent Light* a deceased woman comes back to life. In his book on cinema, Badiou reminds us of the philosophical insistence that the truth is sometimes not the likely. Just to confirm this we then have the final shot of the film: a long immobile take films the sun going down and the slow replacement on-screen of summer evening by starry sky. The other. *Silent Light* illuminates how there can be irruptions of the hitherto unknown. There is something other than what we usually encounter in our diurnal activity. As Castoriadis argues, valuable art, as creation, opens a window upon the chaos, the abyss and the groundless. His examples are *Oedipus Rex*, *Hamlet* and Mozart's *Requiem* but I have sought to show how certain cinematic artworks, as well as other audio-visual forms, can do the uncovering characteristic of great art.

4. Show the chaos of the limits of the narratives we tell ourselves

L'Eclisse – Antonioni (1962). Three circles of chaos. The chaos that lies between the declaration of love and its acknowledgement.

The chaos of the capitalist structure which is in crisis in the film. The chaos of the uncontainable world of the unclosable narrative.

The central scene. Two lovers (Monica Vitti and Alain Delon) meet in the Rome Stock Exchange. They seem to get to know each other but an uncertainty is heightened by the fact that this relationship only has its foundations, if we could call them that, amid the utter over-ritualised capitalist absurdity of the stock exchange – and the question we cannot help asking is: why are they doing this?

The ending of the film. The two main characters have just declared their love for each other: they want to see each other everywhere and as soon as possible. A rather rich (too-rich?) poetic moment for Antonioni. We are then treated to quite a challenging shot as the two lovers stare directly out to us. The Vitti face is pretty unreadable – the Delon face however suggests perhaps some element of insincerity – and this character with his cruelty and untrustworthiness, as shown in his dealings as a kind of stockbroker at other moments in the film, is quite capable of such insincerity. But on the other hand, he could mean it, could possibly be sincere. We just don't know. There follows a sequence in which their afternoon tryst is over and they both start to get back into the workaday world, Vitti pausing as she walks out of the apartment block stairwell, as if realising the love she may feel is without foundation or guarantee or certainty; she seems weakened, bumping clumsily into street strangers. Delon however is restoring his phone network, but is seemingly unable to return to his work pattern. We will never know what they are really feeling because what follows is a disintegration of narrative and a celebration of foundationless form. Seven minutes long.

The last shot of either of the two lovers or indeed of any recognisable character from the film is of Vitti. She walks away.

In the sequence of shots that follows, Antonioni plays with

our desire for narrative event and for recognisable narrative characters. A bus seems to be speeding dangerously, there is a close up on a front wheel, skidding sounds – we think it must be about to crash... but no, it pulls up and some passengers calmly descend. One of them is reading a newspaper warning of weak chances of world peace and nuclear threat – perhaps we ought to be more bothered about these things?

At one point Vitti seems to enter the sequence – we see a head of hair just like hers, which we have seen many times shot from the back during the film – so we think we recognise her. By now our inner narrative drive is demanding some return of narrative sense as this abstract set of images has been running for some time, without explanation. But again we are denied; the head turns to reveal another less architectonic facial structure than that of Vitti's. All of this against a Nono-esque atonality.

Like the water from the barrel that is shown leaking, the narrative just generally disperses; it goes not somewhere, but only to an over-exposed image of a streetlamp resembling the moon – the moon the agent of the eclipse. A stark discord sounds – this is all you are going to get. An astonishing finish which is liberating, it takes you out of the cloying world of the two lovers and shows you chaos, the non-foundations of the story. A window upon the chaos that narrative tends to occult. It says that none of this (this narrative, these stock exchanges) is necessary; all of this is contingent and that is what the lovers have realised, but you must realise it too. There is no necessity to the madness of La Borsa, of an out-of-control, alienating, meaningless capitalism.

5. Show the chaos of the paroxystic

Leviathan – Paravel and Castaing-Taylor (2012). Importantly eschewing the usual generic codes of the documentary, *Leviathan* presents us with a series of images and sounds in which we get the sense of the unseen and unpredictable, the unproducible; a visually paroxystic experience very much akin to Castoriadis' sense of otherness when he notices that what he thought was just a trace of something on a rock moves and he sees that there is a worm there instead. The film begins – a dark screen save some intermittent red glow in the far far right-lower corner of the screen. After a short while blues and greens appear. A series of apparently random sounds humming, flushing and click-clacking. We begin to speculate that some of this sound image pattern may actually be objects, but we are not yet sure. The camera shoots left and for a second we see gloves taking hold of a chain and then back to black. Then – yes – an object, some kind of very green metal crate is pulled up towards us out of the sea. Then the first long shot of a human figure in sea-proof clothing. A world has paroxystically emerged for us. There are other such moments: gleaming white lights in the corner of the screen. They suddenly become recognisable as seagulls tracking the ship. It is important that none of this is set up according to the law of the spectacle. We are not having a paroxystic experience if we are just saying wow. Or even if we are mainly "wowed", for instance when the law of the spectacle prevails even within apparently educational programmes such as David Attenborough's programmes for the BBC. In those programmes we are offered astonishment. This is what distinguishes *Leviathan* from such programmes. In such Attenboroughesque programmes the paroxystic is negated by astonishment. Astonishment tells us that the world is not really full of the new but only of the very rarely new and for that we need our Attenboroughs, our experts, to bring it to view; as such, astonishing spectacles are anti-parox-ystic and anti-democratic.

6. Show the chaos of the disjunction between image and narrative

The Skin I Live In – Almodovar (2011). A film which attends to the effect created when our cognitive channels are presented with contradictory information. The narrative tells us that the woman we see on screen was once a man. The image, on the other hand, seems to not bear this information, so despite the fact that it has been given to us in narrative form – probably the main intuitive mode that humans use to exchange information with each other – there is still massive disjunction. A moment akin to that which fascinates Roland Barthes in *Camera Lucida* is when he looks at the photo of a young man who at the time the photograph was taken had been found guilty of murder and so was going to be killed by the state. Indeed he was put to death – so as Barthes says, he is dead and he going to die. In response to this disjunction Barthes has an attack of "the vertigo of time defeated."[90] Similarly in Almodovar's film we say she is a woman, who was a man, who is going to be a woman, but finally renames themself in masculine form "I'm Vincente" (at the end of the film) and yet in real life – so to speak – we are presented with actress Elena Anaya. Perhaps here we have the vertigo and the chaos of gender defeated.

7. Show the chaos of the object

André Bazin on the long take of the kitchen scene in Welles' *The Magnificent Ambersons*: "The object is always able to remind me of its reality as an object... and the ambivalence of reality."[91] This is Bazin perhaps pre-empting object-oriented ontology by half a century, emphasising the "thingness" of things and a particular ability of the camera, in a very Frammartino way, to open a window onto something that we cannot fully comprehend as human beings. Hence its unbearable nature for Bazin in this shot. We are reminded that the image is not fully ordered. Which convokes a thought and a philosophy of the image; if the image was fully ordered then such Bazinian anguish would not be possible or demanded, and we would have the completion of the film-structuralist dream of scientificity. Fortunately in the 21st century, we have realised that this dream is empty. The materialism of this image from Welles is the index of the unsettledness of being. Through it we can understand the infinity of the real, yet this chaos, this unsettledness, is not simply told to us in a didactic manner. It is, as Badiou insists,

> transmitted through the experience of the vision of film, in its movement: it isn't what is said in the film, it is not the organisation of the intrigue which counts, it is the movement itself which transmits the thought of film.[92]

Conclusion

Here are the key conclusions I reach during the course of the book:

1. What is *is* chaos.
2. The acknowledgement that what is *is* chaos is a necessary condition for the creation of a fully democratic society.
3. Democracy as the political acknowledgement of ontological chaos is anarchic, insurgent and existential.
4. So the way to live life as an existential democratic subject is necessarily to live with and acknowledge ontological chaos.
5. Those who live that life cannot mediate representations of this ontological chaos, but they can create windows upon it.

This book began as a meditation on the concept of the media and the practices which it drives and which I have argued should be ended. "The media" is a notion of suspect provenance whose existence as a mediator, or as mediating, has unfortunately been accepted as an unquestionable truth of our time. But our time is changing. To hasten that change we should dump the concept and the practices that go with it.

We should also create ways of producing images and sounds so that we can create a culture that acknowledges that what is *is* chaos and in order to do that we need, in Castoriadis' term, to create *windows upon the chaos*. To support that, we need new ways of organising the way we produce images and sounds and the institutions that support that production.

Until that time the question is – can producers of sounds and images contribute to existential democratic living? My argument indicates that this is more than eminently possible and is indeed happening. This points towards a fact about the relationship between cultural production and economic organisation. It is possible within capitalism to produce works that criticise and undermine capitalism; we are already communist anarchists in lots of ways and we can make images and sound combinations that embody that engagement.

Here I emphasise that the new is happening – that we have to live life as critical existential subjects open to the new, capable of a certain pensivity, as well as courageous democratic action. The media is against this kind of democratic living but we can create a visual culture that is emancipatory. That visual culture is one where the anarchic, the insurgent and the existential are valued and seen as essential aspects of the democratic.

Democracy Against the Media: Imaginary Fragments from Dixon Street, Stockton-on-Tees, England

In May 2014, an independent television production company went to a town called Stockton-on-Tees, in the North-East of England hoping to start a sequel to their controversial Channel 4 series "Benefits Street" which had been widely condemned for its representations of the working class. They were chased away and pelted with eggs. This postscript sets out a short series of differing imaginary perspectives on that moment.

That day they came to our street they were dressed down in t-shirts and tracksuit bottoms. They said to us that afterwards some of us would get jobs and some of us would profit from it because our house prices would go up. Some of us thought we might get some measure of fame too and that would be pretty cool wouldn't it. Others thought they had accents which were very deserving of respect. They were cut glass in comparison with ours. That must say something. So I agreed to make the series with them.

After it, nothing much changed. I grew old. And from then on my eye was darkened and there was no adventure in my life.

* * *

It was such relief when they turned up that day promising us that just a little bit in the way of cash. My payday loans were getting way too heavy to bear and my mates in Middlesbrough just down the road had said that a money lender I'd moved to avoid had shown them a bullet and said it was for me the next time he saw me. I was pretty desperate. I took the bits and bobs on offer and I featured, which of course put that money lender on my trail straightaway and to be honest with you I had to move not long after.

I had to make sacrifices to make some of the ends meet somehow. Left our lass and the kid behind. I don't really know what became of my daughter. All I heard was that from then on she decided she wanted nothing to do with me.

* * *

My kids would have loved to be on the TV. But there was no way I was going to give in and be filmed and recorded with no say about how it all came out. I'd seen the first series and couldn't believe how some of those people acted up – all for what? In addition I was no stranger to demonstrations and was only too happy when a few of the others said they were ready to join together to do something about it. I know we weren't particularly popular with some of the others in the street but this wasn't about numbers. They'd been taken in by those promises made with that accent. I hadn't, I'd heard that combination many times before and knew they would amount to nothing. Sometimes you just have to do something that others don't understand.

They had wanted to occupy our street and we were the insurgents against the occupation. We didn't absolutely know how it would turn out but we had actually really thought about it and there conditions which led us to make the choice. We took our water and our eggs, we pelted them. They weren't used to this kind of thing. They were used to negotiation, they'd even asked to meet the representative of the state parliament for the area, above our heads. Sensibly he turned them down. They left. Someone had to show them. It felt better than good. It was democracy against the media.

Endnotes

1. BBC interview with Darcus Howe:
   http://www.youtube.com/watch?v=mzDQCT0AJcw
2. Later published research reports into the riots were to confirm that the stop and search police tactics, *as Howe suggested during the interview* were an important factor behind the riots. What is interesting is the mixture of ignorance, incomprehension and antipathy evidenced in the interview by the BBC. The BBC? It is so obviously not just the interviewer herself who embodies these qualities – there is a whole BBC backroom obviously feeding her information and questions down her headphones. "You are not shocked – does this mean that you condone..." (What kind of logic moves from the fact of not being shocked by rioting to condoning it?)
3. Compare this with the laughable suggestion from the Conservative government minister Iain Duncan Smith that the riots were caused by *The X Factor*:
   http://m.guardian.co.uk/uk/2011/dec/09/x-factor-culture-fuelled-riots?cat=uk&type=article
4. Could it be that the BBC cannot tell the difference between a riot and a demonstration? This would be rather anti-democratic of them.
5. The Murdochs give evidence to the select committee:
   https://www.youtube.com/watch?v=AbxE0mPLi7A
6. Jacques Rancière, *Disagreement: Politics and Philosophy*, trans: Julie Rose (Minnesota: University of Minessota Press, 1998), xi.
7. Jacques Rancière, *The Politics of Aesthetics*, trans: Gabriel Rockhill (London: Continuum, 2004), 13.
8. Jacques Rancière, *The Hatred of Democracy*, trans: Steve Corcoran (London: Verso, 2007).

9. Cornelius Castoriadis, *Postscript on Insignificance*, trans: Gabriel Rockhill and John V Garner (London: Continuum, 2011).

10. Miguel Abensour, *Democracy against the State: Marx and The Machiavellian Moment*, trans: Max Blechman and Martin Breaugh (Cambridge: Polity Press, 2011).

11. Jacques Rancière, "L'insurrection démocratique," *Macadam philo 07 – 08, France Culture*: http://www.franceculture.fr/emission-l-insurrection-démocratique-2008-06-27.html

12. Miguel Abensour, *Democracy against the State*.

13. Jean-Luc Nancy, "Finite and Infinite Democracy" in *Democracy in What State*, ed. Giorgio Agamben et al (New York: Columbia UP, 2011).

14. http://www.levesoninquiry.org.uk/

15. Blair advises Brooks before arrest: http://www.bbc.co.uk/news/uk-26259956

16. Asa Briggs and P. Burke, *A Social History of The Media: From Gutenberg to the Internet* (Cambridge: Polity Press, 2002).

17. Castoriadis, *Fenêtre sur le chaos* (Paris: Éditions du Seuil, 2007).

18. If the phrase "the media" is used in what follows, it is in a paradoxical sense. The paradox arises from the fact that this project declares the term should end, yet it still has widespread prevalence and usefully a meaning that broadly designates the production and dissemination of sounds and images.

19. Media Studies has never been particularly acute on the relationship between media and democracy. This becomes evident when we examine academic Media Studies texts where democracy and media are explicitly linked. From the quasi-Habermassian in which democracy is largely assimilated to "consensual democracy" (even in its direct form); to "wonkish" policy-oriented studies where thinking the

unthinkable is bound up in current mainstream politics and its limited sense of democracy; to the semiotic based demotic (if not democratic) privileging of choices of readings begun by the CCCS[i] and continued in most "postmodern" reception theory, and which neglects the force of the image.

20. For a very early critique see: K. McDonnell and K. Robins, *Marxist Cultural Theory: The Althusserian Smokescreen* in *One Dimensional Marxism*, ed. Simon Clarke, Terry Lovell, Kevin McDonnell, Kevin Robins and Victor Selniewski Seidler (London and New York: Alison and Busby, 1980).

21. Chantal Mouffe, *Agonistics: Thinking the World Politically* (London: Verso, 2013).

22. At the moment most Western thought is characterised by what Wilfred Sellars calls "the myth of the given."

23. This is an institutional power which is side-lined or denied by overly optimistic discourses of new media, web 2.0, pick and mix theories of meaning etc. – all of which are central to the recent pedagogy of Media Studies.

24. It seems that a fair few commentators (e.g. http://www.nytimes.com/2011/07/11/business/media/a-tabloid-shame-exposed-by-honest-rivals.html; and http://www.telegraph.co.uk/news/uknews/phone-hacking/8631610/News-of-the-World-phone-hacking-July-11-as-it-happened.html; and http://bloggingheads.tv/diavlogs/37406?in=06:25&out=11:00) were making comparisons between the hacking scandal around News Corporation and its consequences and the revolutions of the Arab Spring. They were calling it the British Spring – even though it was happening in July, the height of what we laughably call summer in Britain. Why isn't it a British Spring? 1. The presumed democratic manifestation is really just a kind of revenge enacted by one

set of corporate bodies (the main British political parties) on others (the corporate bodies of the super (News) Corporation) most unlike the genuine popular manifestations of the Arab Spring. 2. The likely outcomes are paltry in comparison to real revolutionary outcomes: the closure of a valueless and toxic newspaper, only to be replaced by a slightly altered version a few months later; News Corp maintaining a major controlling share in BSkyB; a few changes in personnel at the top of News Corp; probably very little in terms of changes in media regulation or media practices. Why will there be little change in media regulation? Well, why would the Tory party change its corporate profiteerism?

25. "It was only in the 1920s – according to the Oxford English Dictionary – that people began to speak of the media." G. Snow, "Briggs and Burke's History of the Media," in *Advertising & Selling* v. 240, ed. N. T. Praigg. Mass media represents the most economical way of getting the story over the new and wider market in the least time.

26. *Philosophie du vivre* (Paris: Éditions Gallimard, 2011).

27. "C'est clair: ils sonts soulagés d'avoir évité d'affronter – affronter ce qui se présentait à eux, engouffrant leur attention, et de toutes parts les débordait."

28. *Philosophie du vivre*, p. 20-24.

29. I have merged Jullien's translation with one of the English translations. There are other translations, for example: "Those unmindful when they hear, for all they make of their intelligence, may be regarded as the walking dead." (Fragment 3, Penguin Classics, 2001)

30. Interview on DVD, *Le Quattro Volte*

31. See Chapter Two of this book for a development of this line of thought.

32. There is a consonance between Badiou and Jullien's work – Badiou refers to "l'extreme importance, la nouveauté, la

fécondité, des recherches diagonales de Jullien" (See Badiou's essay, "Jullien: l'apostat," in *Oser Construire: Pour François Jullien de Pierre Chartier Empêcheurs de Penser en Rond (2007)*).

33. Alain Badiou, *Being and Event* (Continuum: London, 2011).
34. http://themediaagainstdemocracy.wordpress.com/2012/07/03/the-anarchic-art-of-hilary-lloyd/
35. http://thereturnofthepublic.wordpress.com/2012/07/03/the-bbc-governance-structure-at-a-glance/;
    and
    http://www.suttontrust.com/news/news/over-half-the-countrys-top-journalists-went-to-private-schools/
36. Alternatively take a purely market phenomenon such as the broadcasters like ITV and C5 – in what sense could they be regarded as really democratic? The meaning of democracy is fully discussed in Chapter Three of this book. As Rousseau says, "the will cannot be represented" (*The Social Contract Book 3*, chapter 15, (Penguin: London, 2012)).
37. http://www.guardian.co.uk/media/2005/apr/11/broadcasting.mondaymediasection;
    and
    http://www.theweek.co.uk/politics/20733/how-media-became-painfully-middle-class
38. Why is it that porn images rather than porn writing shock us? Why is it that "smoking kills" does not get to us as much as images of rotting gums? Why do we have national bodies regulating images but not words e.g. BBFC? Why can you get put in prison for simply viewing certain images (and even if the images are not "real" images)? It is not because of meaning although clearly meaning is important. It is because images always have something else in them other than their capacity to produce meaning even if that capacity can have polysemic richness. In privileging meaning and the epistemological over experience and the ontological, Media

Studies has misunderstood what images and sounds do and can do.

39. See the last chapter of this book for more on that.

40. Georg Simmel (quoted by Abensour in *Democracy against the State*).

41. Miguel Abensour, *Democracy against the State*.

42. Francois Jullien, *Philosophie du vivre*.

43. As Evelyne Pieiller asks in her review of Jullien's work in *Le Monde Diplomatique*, August 2011: "Comment être présent au monde? Comment conserver ce sentiment de plénitude qui surgit sans prévenir, et met au centre la joie d'exister, tandis que s'estompent les exigences de l'égo?"

44. Why is such thinking often accompanied by a sense of exhilaration? Think of the artworks that attract us all the more when they invite us to think of our death. Isn't this one of the reasons why thought associated with the existential – Sartre, Camus etc. – took hold of the popular-intellectual imagination and still does grip us?

45. In order to set out a convincing case for the overall thesis of this book it is necessary that I set out Meillassoux's argument for hyper-chaos, which I rely upon. I then want to press on to some of the consequences of Meillassoux's work in order to suggest ways in which sound and image culture may be able to get an aperture onto this ontological chaos or hyper-chaos. There are already adequate and interesting book-length accounts of Meillassoux's thought (Harman and Ennis) although both of them were published before Meillassoux's crucial lecture in Berlin in 2012, in which he clarified his thinking and before the publication of Meillassoux's fascinating account of Mallarmé's poem *A Throw of the Dice Will Never Abolish Chance*. I am referring to his book *The Number and The Siren*.

46. Meillassoux, *After Finitude: An Essay on the Necessity of Contingency* (Bloomsbury Academic: London, 2010).

47. Meillassoux wavers on this point. In *AF* he uses "hyper-chaos," in his interview with Graham Harman Quentin he tries out "super-chaos" (*Philosophy in the Making*, Edinburgh University Press, 2011, p.162), but then in Berlin in 2012 he goes back to "hyper-chaos."

48. Developments in theoretical physics support this philosophical work. Joseph Lykken has said that "What happens is you get just a quantum fluctuation that makes a tiny bubble of the vacuum the Universe really wants to be in. And because it's a lower-energy state, this bubble will then expand, basically at the speed of light, and sweep everything before it." http://www.bbc.co.uk/news/science-environment -21499765

    Fellow theoretical physicist Gian Giudice supports this point about the instability of the universe: http://www.ted.com/talks/gian_giudice_why_our_universe _might_exist_on_a_knife_edge.

49. There are many adequate expositions of Meillassoux's work available and so I hope the reader will forgive my concentrated account of his speculative materialism.

50. There seems like a big leap to the final astonishing concluding sentence from the rest of the argument. What could bridge the two? We are here facing up to a criticism that has been made of Meillassoux by Peter Hallward (see next footnote): that Meillassoux equivocates between the ontological and the epistemological.

    He doesn't – although perhaps we can better see that he doesn't following his unpublished Berlin lecture of 2012, made *after* Hallward's criticism. Following this lecture we can see that there was an ambiguity or difficulty with the notion of correlation which caused a problem. The correlation is initially seemingly coined as a term that relates to epistemology – the idea that its critique leads to a realism in the form of speculative realism is one of the consequences of this kind of thinking about what the correlate as a term might mean. But Meillassoux specifically distances himself from the speculative realist term. He is not a speculative realist, he states in the Berlin lecture of 2012, but rather a speculative materialist – this is a rather less epistemological term and much more an ontological term, and by insisting on this term he is stating that he is primarily an ontological thinker.

How is this ontological primacy manifested in Meillassoux's thought? In his key work, *After Finitude*, and in some subsequent publications, Meillassoux surveys a variety of epistemological positions but ultimately finds them all problematical. The reason he finds them all problematical is that the epistemological problem that they are trying and failing to address needs a more rigorous *ontological* thinking. So now we can reconsider the idea that Meillassoux equivocates between epistemology and ontology, and see that rather than an equivocation between the two there is an interrogation of the epistemological, via the ontological, and this interrogation is one where the ontological and the epistemological are very closely related. He insists that if we think the epistemological problems from an ontological perspective then we can clear up some of the *aporia* and paradoxes that have dogged the philosophical tradition (Hume's problem of induction is one such, which Meillassoux takes up in his paper *Potentiality and Virtuality*).

As we have seen, Meillassoux discovers that our knowledge of the world, our epistemology, is dependent upon using the correlation – which is a thing – and so when we are using the correlation we are involved in an activity which is properly understood via the ontological, we are positing that what is *is* characterised by its being intermingled with thought.

51. Peter Hallward, "Anything is Possible," *Radical Philosophy*, no.152, 2008, pp. 55. But also see Nathan Brown's essay in the

collection *The Speculative Turn* (Melbourne: Re.Press, 2011), p.143. Another criticism that Hallward makes of Meillassoux is that his is an "acausal ontology, in other words, includes no account of an actual process of transformation or development. There is no account here of any positive ontological or historical force, no substitute for what other thinkers have conceived as substance, or spirit, or power, or labour"; and that "His insistence that anything might happen can only amount to an insistence on the bare possibility of radical change."

I am not sure that this can only amount to a bare possibility of change but certainly the political consequences of this kind of ontology are under-theorised in Meillassoux's work – but on the other hand, how many books are we asking him to write? However it will be my argument that this notion of ontological chaos can be further theorised and developed and that Castoriadis' philosophy is helpful in this regard by helping us think the political beyond an insistence on concepts depending upon heteronomous "forces of history" which are potentially anti-democratic and anti-emancipatory and lend themselves to an ultimately useless cultish Marxism. So my next chapter will outline how Castoriadis' work can help us understand the nature of chaos and why the political acknowledgement of it is necessary but of course not sufficient for emancipation.

52. "Institution of Society and Religion" in *World in Fragments* (Stanford: Stanford University Press, 1997).

53. "The Imaginary: Creation in the Social-Historical Domain" in *World in Fragments*.

54. My dictionary echoes Castoriadis in telling that an obsolete meaning of chaos links it to the ideas of chasm and abyss.

55. Castoriadis, *Faux et vrai chaos* (Paris: Editions du Seuil, 1999).

56. "The Meaning of Existence and The Contingency of Sense," *Speculations: A Journal of Speculative Realism* IV (2013),

http://speculations-journal.org. Gabriel also gives a very clear and engaging TED talk on this subject: http://www.youtube.com/watch?v=hzvesGB_TI0.

57. See also from another kind of philosophy Derek Parfitt's work on this.

58. See Kevin Robins' 1996 essay "Interrupting Identities: Turkey/Europe" in *Questions of Cultural Identity*. Eds Stuart Hall and Paul du Gay (Sage, 1996).

59. Castoriadis, "Anthropology Philosophy Politics," *Thesis Eleven*, Number 49 (May 1997): 99-116.

60. Roy Brassier, "Concepts and Objects" in *The Speculative Turn: Continental Realism and Materialism*. Eds Levi Bryant, Nick Srnicek and Graham Harman, (Melbourne: Re.Press, 2011).

61. Castoriadis, "Time and Creation" in *World in Fragments*, trans. David Ames Curtis. (Stanford: Stanford UP, 1997).

62. Rene Char: "Comment vivre sans l'inconnu devant soi."

63. Meillassoux, "Potentiality and Virtuality" in *The Speculative Turn* (Melbourne: Re.Press, 2011).

64. If this is true then all sorts of new philosophical paths start opening up, ones that could lead to new solutions to age-old philosophical *aporia*. For example, we can create a new theory of free will based on Meillassoux. We act freely most of the time because there are multiple always-happening *virtual* thought-events and they are caused by humans. Humans have a special relationship with time – we are (in) time and we can think in time – this is a primary quality of consciousness. And consciousness is virtual – and I wish to lend to this word the meaning it has from its epistemological root as possessing certain virtues i.e. it is virtuous, with virtue being not just an excellence but a power; it is a strength which humans have. The advent of logical thought itself was a virtual event and each new singular thought is also itself a new virtual event. The more creative the thought the more virtual it is (virtual here, as I said, is linked to the

root, signifying strength). We can speak of the power of poetry, the power of the created image and sound, and lastly the power of philosophy – perhaps this is what the continental tradition has always been close to. The creation of images and sounds gains its value through their relationship to Meillassouxian chaos. For Meillassoux there are potentialities which are probabilistic and virtualities which are not (see Harman's interview with him in *Philosophy in the Making*). Virtualities just occur without us being able to know their probability – not for epistemological lack on our part as in chaos theory but because of ontological hyperchaos. If we affix to this Badiou's notion of the subject as the being that is seized by and affirms an event, here recast and understood as an advent, then this begins to look like a sort of compatibilism. We cannot control the appearance of a virtuality but we can and sometimes do affirm it.

65. Ray Brassier has expressed concern about the growth of religious concepts in recent ontological thought.

66. Friedrich Nietzsche, *Beyond Good and Evil*, trans. Ian Johnston Richer (Virginia: Resources Publications, 2009).

67. Gilles Deleuze, *Difference and Repetition* (London: Continuum, 2004).

68. Simon Critchley, *Infinitely Demanding* (London: Verso, 2012).

69. Rancière, "The Pensive Image," *The Emancipated Spectator*, trans. Gregory Elliot (London: Verso, 2009).

70. Ibid.

71. Some might say we must look at what professed anarchists have said about democracy. A survey of such opinion, as set out in Robert Graham's *Anarchism: From Anarchy to Anarchism (300CE to 1939) v. 1: A Documentary History of Libertarian Ideas* (Black Rose Books, 2005), reveals a range of opinions stretching from the positively affirmative through ambivalence to absolute antipathy. So Proudhon discusses "democracy in so far as it implies any government at all." Or

Anselm Bellegarrigue: "Thus anarchy, which when contrasted with the term monarchy, means civil war, is, from the vantage point of absolute or democratic truth, nothing less than the true expression of social order." Bellegarrigue here implies that democracy and anarchy are symbiotic. Pujols advocated a collectivist form of anarchism, based on direct democracy.

Alternatively there is that strand in anarchistic thinking that seems opposed to democracy. Malatesta defines democracy as "majority government." Leval challenges Malatesta's view of democracy by discussing the notion of "true democracy." Implying that there are true and false democracies, perhaps Herbert Read was thinking of true democracy when as a professed anarchist, he discusses "a democracy of vital artic-ulation and efficient force."

So in anarchist discourse it is not at all simply the case that democracy and anarchy are opposed to each other: sometimes they are strongly, symbiotically linked; at other times there is ambiguity about their relationship; at again another moment there is some direct opposition but then that opposition is called into question by the implication that democracy is a contested term, that there might be false and true versions of it and that anarchy could embrace true democracy.

72. The political struggle is also the struggle for the appropri-ation of words. There is an old philosophical dream, which analytic philosophy still keeps alive, of defining the meanings of words with such perfection as to make ambiguity and multiple meanings vanish (Rancière in the collection of essays on the meaning of democracy: *Democracy in what state?* Columbia UP, 2011).

73. Badiou, *La pornographie du temps present* (Paris: Fayard, 2013).

74. Daniel Colson, *Petit lexique philosophique de l'anarchisme.* (De Proudhon à Deleuze Le Livre, 2001).

75. Josiah Ober, "The Original Meaning of 'Democracy': Capacity to Do Things, not Majority Rule." *Constellations*, vol. 15, no. 1, 2008. It is also at this point worth noting that neither Ober nor I are arguing for a purely etymological source as the true meaning and Ober is explicit on this: "Of course, we are not bound by any past convention, much less by the inventors' original definition: if we can devise a better meaning for a political term, it should be preferred. But if common modern usages are not particularly good, in the sense of being 'descriptively accurate' or 'normatively choiceworthy,' then there may be some value in returning to the source."

76. "La démocratie insurgeante n'est pas une variante de la démocratie conflictuelle, mais son exact opposé. Tandis que la démocratie conflictuelle pratique le conflit à l'intérieur de l'Etat, de l'Etat démocratique qui donne son nom même se donne comme un évitement du conflit premier, inclinant du même coup la conflictualité vers le compromis permanent, la démocratie insurgeante situe le conflit dans un autre lieu, à l'extérieur de l'Etat, contre lui, et bien loin de pratiquer l'évitement du conflit majeur, – la démocratie contre l'Etat." (Miguel Abensour, *La Démocratie contre l'Etat: Marx et le moment machiavélien* (Broché, 2004): 18-19).

77. "La démocratie insurgeante prend naissance dans l'intuition qu'il n y a pas de vraie démocratie sans réactiver l'impulsion profonde de la démocratie contre toute forme d'arché, impulsion anarchique qui se dresse donc en priorité contre la manifestation classique de l'arché – à savoir, l'Etat."

78. "Au lieu de concevoir l'émancipation comme la victoire du social (une société civile réconciliée) sur le politique, entraînant du même coup la disparition du politique, cette forme de démocratie fait surgir, travaille a faire surgir en permanence, une communauté politique contre l'Etat. A l'opposition du social et du politique, elle substitue celle du

politique et de l'étatique."

79. "Détrônant l'Etat, elle dresse le politique contre l'étatique et rouvre l'abîme trop souvent occulté entre le politique et l'Etat."

80. "A démocratie est le théâtre d'une insurrection permanente contre l'Etat, contre la forme Etat, unificatrice, intégratrice, organisatrice."

81. Rancière, "Does Democracy Mean Something?" in *Rancière Dissensus: On Politics and Aesthetics*, ed. and trans. Steven Corcoran (London: Continuum, 2010).

82. Nancy, "Finite and Infinite Democracy" in *Democracy in What State*, ed. Giorgio Agamben et al (New York: Columbia UP, 2011).

83. Frank Webster, *Theories of the Information Society*, 3rd Edition (Routledge, 2006).

84. Rancière: "Democracy initially stirred up political philosophy because it is not a set of institutions or one kind of regime amongst others but a way for politics to be. Democracy is not the parliamentary system or the legitimate State" (*Disagreement: Politics and Philosophy*, trand. Julie Rose (U of Minnesota P, 2004)).

85. Rancière, *The Hatred of Democracy*, (London: Verso, 2009). "The idea of the republic is one of a system of institutions, laws and moral values that eliminate democratic excess by making State and society homogenous."

86. Ibid.

87. "La démocratie sait-elle favoriser cet acte de rébellion, de révolte intérieure qui est au cœur de la grande littérature et de l'art?" (Interview with George Steiner in *Le Monde*, 2013).

88. Castoriadis, *Fenêtre sur le chaos* (Seuil, 2007).

89. Ibid. "Le chaos est au-déla ou en déçà toute signification. L'être n'a de signification que pour les théologiques: c'est Dieu, c'est le monde crée par Dieu pour nous... Mais le sens de l'a-sensé et l'a-sensé du sens cela veut dire quoi?"

90. Roland Barthes, *Camera Lucida*, trans. Richard Howard (Vintage Classics, 1993).
91. André Bazin, *Orson Welles* (Paris: Chavane, 1950).
92. Badiou, Alain: *Cinema* (London: Polity Press, 2013).

Contemporary culture has eliminated both the concept of the
public and the figure of the intellectual. Former public spaces –
both physical and cultural – are now either derelict or colonized
by advertising. A cretinous anti-intellectualism presides,
cheerled by expensively educated hacks in the pay of
multinational corporations who reassure their bored readers
that there is no need to rouse themselves from their interpassive
stupor. The informal censorship internalized and propagated by
the cultural workers of late capitalism generates a banal
conformity that the propaganda chiefs of Stalinism could only
ever have dreamt of imposing. Zer0 Books knows that another
kind of discourse – intellectual without being academic, popular
without being populist – is not only possible: it is already
flourishing, in the regions beyond the striplit malls of so-called
mass media and the neurotically bureaucratic halls of the
academy. Zer0 is committed to the idea of publishing as a
making public of the intellectual. It is convinced that in
the unthinking, blandly consensual culture in which we live,
critical and engaged theoretical reflection is more important
than ever before.